DELTA TEACHER DEVELOPMENT SERIES

Series editors Mike Burghall and Lindsay Clandfield

Teaching Online

Tools and techniques, options and opportunities

Nicky Hockly with Lindsay Clandfield

Published by
DELTA PUBLISHING
Quince Cottage
Hoe Lane
Peaslake
Surrey GU5 9SW
England

www.deltapublishing.co.uk

© Delta Publishing 2010

First published 2010

ISBN 978-1-905085-35-4

Edited by Mike Burghall
Designed by Christine Cox
Cover photo © iStockphoto.com/Robert Churchill
Printed by Halstan & Co., Amersham, Bucks, England

Nicky would like to dedicate this book to her long-time
friend and colleague Gavin Dudeney, from whom she has
learnt so much about all things technical over the past
decade.

Lindsay's father, David Clandfield, bought a Macintosh
computer when Lindsay was thirteen years old and let him
use it. The computer skills acquired at that age have helped
him immensely in his teaching, writing and online career.
This book is for him.

Acknowledgements

Everything that we have learned about online teaching and
learning has been as part of a team. We both work with The
Consultants-E, an online teacher training and development
organisation. It has been the input, ideas and support of our
Consultants-E colleagues that has helped us both learn and
develop online. Rather than mention individual names, we
would refer you to our website, where you can read about
these very experienced and outstanding online practitioners:
http://www.theconsultants-e.com/courses/tutors

And of course we also owe a huge debt of gratitude to all
the teachers, from all over the world, who have done online
courses with us, and with whom we have used many of the
activities described in this book.

Special thanks go to editor Mike Burghall for his excellent
help and support in shaping this book, and to designer
Christine Cox for bringing her prowess to bear on every
page.

From the authors

It feels like a very long time ago, but in fact it was only 1997. Those were the early days of Virtual Learning Environments (VLEs), and I cut my teeth writing materials and tutoring on an online MA programme.

I learned the hard way. I'm primarily an educator, a face-to-face language teacher and teacher trainer. I knew next to nothing about technology back then. Apart from a technician in a T-shirt telling me (far too fast) how our online platform worked, I had absolutely no training.

Suddenly I found myself running this full MA programme online, with real students, and it was sink or swim. I don't think I exactly swam gold medal style but I managed to keep my head above water, although it cost me many sleepless nights. The course had no classroom component at all. As a face-to-face trainer, I knew it was important to get the group to gel online, and I also had to help my learners find their way around the VLE – all at a distance.

Where to start? What to do? How to design interactive and meaningful tasks for my learners? How to make the whole experience enjoyable for them and for me? How to keep us all afloat – for two whole years? I really didn't know. Nevertheless, for six months I survived and the group seemed to be coming along fine.

Then things changed. I took a six-week fully-online course run by a university in the UK.

A revelation! As a learner on a well-designed online course, I learned more in six weeks than in six months on my own. Not only important things about task design but, more importantly, I had the experience of being an online learner myself. It was a real eye-opener.

Although I consider myself an independent and self-motivated learner, I started to realise just how important tutor support is online, how a fast response time is fundamental, how being heard and responded to by both tutor and peers is vital, how tasks can be meaningful and collaborative. And praise! I needed praise from my tutor. Lots of it!

That's why Lindsay and I got together to write this book. Because, even now, there are still many of you out there who are asked to provide learners with online and blended (partly online) learning, but are given no support. You may get technical help with the VLE, but you often get no pedagogical support at all. We hope this book will provide it.

In 2003, my boss asked me to look into setting up a distance-learning component to our teacher training courses. I thought that this would simply involve putting material onto our website for students to download and read, and preparing a few assignments to go with it. The little distance learning I had done myself had been more or less that – the students were sent material, worked through it, sent it back; the tutor gave them a mark (and perhaps feedback).

I had heard of a new consultancy for teachers that specialised in online teaching, and I convinced my boss to let me do a course 'just in case there was anything we should know'. This was one of the first courses in e-moderation that Nicky and her colleague Gavin Dudeney were offering. My eyes were opened.

I realised there was far more to teaching online than providing input and expecting output in a series of one-way interactions. I learned how to navigate my way around a VLE. But I also learned how to create a group dynamic in which all the participants communicate with each other and learn from each other. I learned about motivation in online learning, and about the high rate of dropout on online courses that was sadly the norm for many institutions that did not properly deal with the medium of the internet and education. And all this was done 100% online.

I walked into my boss's office and said 'We have to completely rethink how we are going to do our online teaching'.

Since then, I have run numerous courses completely online, joined Nicky's consultancy and trained other teachers in e-moderation. It has been a very exciting seven years, as more and more tools appeared that can be harnessed for teaching. When Nicky asked me if I would like to contribute to a book containing all the techniques and activities she had developed over the years, I was delighted. It is always a pleasure to collaborate and work with one's teacher and mentor.

Teaching online is not the future anymore. It is an important part of the here and now of language teaching education. Teachers need to know what tools are out there and what techniques can help them to use these tools. We hope this book will provide support in a positive and practical way.

So if your boss tells you to start teaching some of your classes online, don't panic! You have in your hands a useful guide – to start, or further develop, your *Teaching Online*.

Contents

Contents

Hardware

Here are the basic elements of hardware that you need to get started with online teaching.
It is a good idea to have at least four of the five (a digital camera is optional).
They provide the bricks and mortar of your online course.

Internet connection

Broadband internet access is faster and more efficient than analogue (or 'dial-up') access. Good internet access is important if you are going to use audio and video on your online courses.

Microphone/speakers or headset

Your laptop may have a built-in microphone and speakers, but a headset with a USB plug will give you better quality sound. This is important if you are going to speak to your learners online.

Computer

You can use a desktop computer, a laptop computer or a tablet computer. Most computers (especially laptops) now come with all of the elements on this page.

Webcam

You can buy a webcam for your desktop computer. Your laptop may have one built-in. When you use your webcam to record yourself, or to video-conference with your learners, make sure you have a light in front of you (eg next to your computer screen) so your face is not in the dark!

Digital camera (optional)

Digital cameras are affordable these days, and can be used to take photos for a variety of online activities and projects. Your mobile phone may include one.

Teaching online

Online learning is becoming increasingly popular, both in the field of language teaching and in mainstream education. Online course delivery has now been around for well over a decade, and we are getting to the point where learners often expect some sort of online component or support as part of their course. Many teachers are embracing this new form of course delivery as an opportunity. And just as many teachers perceive the move towards online courses as an ordeal, a threat or at least a source of stress.

There is also growing pressure on both teachers and institutions to offer their learners online learning options to supplement f2f (face-to-face) classes, due not only to the spectacular growth of technology and increased access to it over the last decade, but also due to the increasingly busy lifestyles of our adult learners and the increased 'tech-savviness' of our younger learners.

We have come across many teachers in our work who admit quite openly that they are 'terrified' of having to teach online, even though they do recognise the potential advantages for their learners.

Ordeal or opportunity?

Whether you perceive online learning as an *opportunity* or an *ordeal* will depend to a large extent on how well prepared you are to deal with this new form of teaching and learning. And this is where we hope this book can help – by preparing you for online teaching.

But first things first.

When exactly might you offer online learning to your learners? Let us begin by imagining four different situations:

- You are a freelance English teacher.
- You are the director of studies of a language school.
- You are a teacher in a university language department.
- You teach younger learners up to the age of 16.

Before you read on and turn the page, you might like to stop and think of some of the variables within each of these situations. Putting yourself into these positions may provoke different feelings. For many, perhaps the second scenario makes an online option seem like an immediate opportunity. It is flexible, it is potentially cheaper and it is new and exciting for many teachers. However, looking at the other situations, the option can seem more like an ordeal. Will you know as much about technology as your young learners, for example?

Learners often expect some sort of online component or support as part of their course.

We hope this book can help – by preparing you for online teaching.

Ongoing opportunities

The modern world of English language teaching is a web of interconnected needs and knowledge.

The modern world of language teaching is a web of interconnected needs and knowledge, where private and public, providers and pedagogues, teachers and learners all need to evolve and evaluate their options and obligations, their immediate possibilities and their long-term potential. Nowadays, much of this can take place online.

Let's look at our four educational scenarios and endeavour to see them in a positive light, envisaging the multiple online opportunities they can afford.

1 As a **freelance English teacher**, you hold business English classes in a large company several times a week. Your learners are all middle managers in the company, so they are extremely busy and often miss classes …

- Why not teach these learners fewer hours face-to-face and set them work online, so that they can complete some of the work at their own pace?
- Why not provide them with extra resources online in their particular area of work – in English? Links to articles, websites, videos, audio or video podcasts: they can all give your learners relevant exposure to language outside the classroom.
- Why not deliver some of your course content via a VLE (Virtual Learning Environment), which allows for detailed learner tracking. See exactly what work they have done, collate their grades and participation, then use this information to generate reports on their contribution to your course and share it with the Human Resources department of the company (with the learners´ knowledge and consent of course!).

2 You are the **director of studies** of a language school. Times have been difficult recently, and many of your classrooms are empty. You have a computer room, but it's not used much by the teachers. One day you read an article about Virtual Learning Environments, the platforms which can be used to deliver courses online. You know that many potential students have an internet connection …

- What about surveying the learners at your school to gauge to what extent they would like to have more classes online?
- What about having a free Virtual Learning Environment installed on your school computer server for practically nothing (or hosting it externally very cheaply)?
- What about offering extra learning resources online for your exam classes – a highly effective marketing, and not only educational, strategy – as added value to exam preparation?

3 You are a **teacher in a university** language department. You have had access to the computer room in the past, but you have never really bothered taking learners there often, partly because you aren't entirely sure about how to use the equipment. One day, in a department meeting, it is announced that all courses at the university will have an online component. Teachers will have to deliver twenty percent of their language courses via the internet. You are 'invited' to be part of a small group to design the online curriculum – and the first course begins in a few weeks …

Look at the elements of your curriculum which can most easily and effectively be delivered online.

- You can make contact with colleagues in other institutions who may have already gone through a similar experience. How? By joining an online teacher development group and asking for help and advice. There are many professionals in our field out here who are happy to share their (often considerable) experience and insights.
- You can start small. Look at the elements of your curriculum which can most easily and effectively be delivered online, and prepare those for online delivery. Use this book as a guide!
- You can get yourself some training, at the same time as working on your online curriculum. Either in-house or externally, face-to-face (f2f) or online – if you are inexperienced in an area, (good) training is tremendously helpful.

4 You teach **younger learners** in a state school or perhaps a language school. Your learners seem to know a lot about technology, and use tools such as Facebook, instant messaging and MP3 players in their spare time. You know that they are extremely motivated by technical things, and so you would like to start incorporating some of these tools into your teaching …

- How about starting to use more technology in your classroom by using internet-based materials such as videos, film clips or instant translation tools? Part B of *Teaching Online* provides you with activities that can be done online but can also be carried out in the f2f classroom.
- How about encouraging your learners to use more technology in their homework assignments? Instead of a hand-written piece of work, get them to contribute to a class blog or wiki, or produce their own short movies or audio clips on their mobile phones.
- How about organising a class 'show and tell', where the learners share videos or photos they have created or taken? You may be surprised to learn that 'A' has advanced audio or video editing skills or that 'B' likes playing around with photo effects. They can show their artefacts to the rest of the class and you will get a good idea of the interests and technology skills in the class as a whole. You then use the more tech-savvy learners to help you to handle the technological aspects of a class project!

> Teachers will not implement all the occasions for online teaching immediately.

Obviously, teachers will not implement all the occasions for online teaching and learning immediately. It is a more a question of *ongoing* development, both personal and professional.

Online learning

It is our hope that *Teaching Online* will provide some of the answers to some of the questions you will certainly be asking. It may be useful at this point, therefore, to clarify some terms.

Online learning

This is, in the strictest sense, learning that takes place using a computer connected to the internet as a tool for communication and learning. There has been much misuse of the term:

> We take the term 'online learning' to include using computer-based tools which promote an element of communication and interactivity.

- Self-study tools such as CD-ROMs have been called online learning.
- In this book we take the term to include using computer-based tools which promote an element of *communication* and *interactivity* with other people, either learners and/or teachers.

After all, learning a language requires communication with other human beings, not just with a computer program!

Blended learning

Here we have another increasingly frequently used term:

- It refers to a mixture of both face-to-face and online learning – some elements of a course are delivered online, and some are delivered f2f.
- The ratio of online to f2f course delivery can vary greatly, as we shall see, from 100% online to any combination of f2f and online.

> Current research suggests that the best results come from offering learners a blended option.

While everyone agrees that technology and online options are here to stay, opinions about the benefits of purely online learning are divided. An exclusively online option – where 100% of a course for learning a language is offered online – *is* possible, and there are in fact online language schools in existence. But current research suggests that the best results in most disciplines come from offering learners a *blended* option – that is, part of the teaching is offered online and part face-to-face. Indeed, it appears that combining online elements with f2f elements means that learners do even better than in purely f2f learning.

Opinions

To what extent, then, is learning online a good thing or a bad thing? Well, as with anything in life, there are benefits and drawbacks. We have summarised some of the advantages and disadvantages of online learning below:

☺	☹
Flexible – learners can log on when and where they like.	Flexibility means learners need to be disciplined and self-motivated.
Learners have access all day, every day.	Learners may expect the teacher to be available 24/7.
It is quick and easy for learners to submit work and assignments.	Learners may expect instant responses and feedback.
Geographical location is not an issue.	It may be difficult to meet in real-time across time zones.
Many learners are familiar with the internet already.	Some learners may find working online alienating, or spend too much time already online at work.
It can include multimedia.	Lower-bandwidth connections can mean that not all media can be viewed easily.
It can be cheaper for the learner.	It can be more time-consuming for teachers.

Our feeling is that the advantages of online learning far outweigh the disadvantages.

Our feeling as educators is that the advantages of the left column far outweigh the disadvantages on the right. With training, practice and ideas:

- Teachers can create online learning opportunities.
- Teachers can have learners practise all four skills online.
- Teachers can create enjoyable and memorable group experiences.

So don't worry! You're off to a good start just reading this book. We aim to show you how to offer any part (or even all!) of your language courses online, by pointing you towards the tools and techniques that we have found work best.

Organisation

Teaching a course online isn't an all-or-nothing thing. As we shall see, blended learning is a popular (and effective) option for many courses. For those new to both teaching and learning online it may offer a good solution. How does it work in practice? The following are all examples of organising different online options, or blended learning scenarios:

Online work can be individual work, but often requires the learners to work in pairs or small groups, using internet-based tools.

- Learners have two English classes a week – one class is f2f, the other class requires them to do work from home or work using a computer. The online work can be individual work, but often requires the learners to work in pairs or small groups at a distance, using internet-based tools to complete project work covering a range of skills.
- Learners on a one-year English course meet f2f once a month to practise speaking skills with the class and the teacher. The rest of the month's work is carried out via the computer, both in collaborative groups and individually, with teacher feedback and support.
- Learners on an intensive English course have five or six hours of class a day. For an hour a day they spend time in the computer lab, working on computers. This hour does not involve only using self-study CD-ROMs, but also internet-based communicative project work which practises a wide range of skills.

- Learners who are in different countries or regions have an initial period of time working on a range of language skills from home with fellow learners and the teacher via a Virtual Learning Environment. They eventually meet for a period of time face-to-face, after having worked together online over several months. Or perhaps an initial f2f meeting period is followed by several months of online work in a VLE.

As we see from these short scenarios, a blended learning course will typically be organised partly face-to-face and partly online – and the online delivery frequently takes place at a distance. Most importantly, the online component still offers opportunities for interaction and communication between learners, and between learners and teacher. Finally, as in a traditional f2f language course, a range of skills is covered in the course (although only some skills may be covered online and some f2f): you may want to work on your learners' speaking skills exclusively f2f, for example.

Openings

Let us think back to the situations we outlined at the beginning of these pages. Have you ever found yourself in one of these situations?

- How do teachers get involved in teaching online?
- What doors can online teaching open?

We have seen a growth of teachers who will need to be online for some of their teaching work.

We have seen a growth of teachers who will need to be online for some of their teaching work. Some may be interested in technology and keen to try out new approaches in their teaching, so start to offer their learners blended options – these 'early adopters' of technology, however, tend to be in the minority. Other teachers many find themselves having to introduce elements of online learning because their institution has decided to offer this to learners. Still others may find that offering online components of a course is part of a wider Ministry of Education decision in their context.

Finally, there are the teachers who see new career openings and decide that they would like to become online tutors and to spend more time working from home, whether for professional or personal reasons. Often these are freelance teachers, who would like to offer their private learners online and blended learning options as a 'unique selling point' or in order to expand their repertoire of teaching skills.

Objectives

There are some initial questions to ask yourself when designing and delivering your blended or online course.

Whatever the reasons for deciding to include an online component in your teaching, there are some initial questions to ask yourself when you come to designing and delivering your blended or online course, and the answers will depend on what your objectives are – the outcomes you are seeking.

How much online?

First of all, *how much* of your course will be online? If you have a regular f2f course you could start by only putting between 10% and 20% online. So if you teach a class for three hours a week, you could get your learners to do one hour's worth of classwork online once every two weeks.

What online?

Now you need to ask yourself exactly *what parts* of your course could best be offered online. Are you going to get your learners to do grammar work online? Or perhaps some reading, writing or listening? If you are using a coursebook, perhaps choose the parts that can most easily be delivered online, such as the writing activities. Or you could offer some extra listening and grammar activities for your learners. We provide plenty of ideas for online activities for these and other skills in Part B of this book.

How online?

You then need to think about *how* you are going to offer the online part of your course. Are you going to send your learners emails with links, documents and instructions for their online work? Or are you going to use a range of internet-based tools such as blogs and wikis, or even a VLE? We suggest that you go beyond email – by using a range of free tools available on the internet, you will give your learners a far better learning experience.

We will be looking in detail at the tools available for teachers, and we will be providing suggestions on how you might use them with your learners. At this point, we would certainly suggest you make a decision to use a range of tools, and not restrict yourself to just email.

Once you have clear answers for these key questions, you're ready to design your course.

By using a range of free tools available on the internet, you will give your learners a far better learning experience.

Overview

The first thing to do is to ensure that you have an overview of what you are going to do f2f, and what you are going to do online. First, make a blank course plan in the form of a grid.

Below is a blank course plan for the first two weeks of a language course, in which the learners meet for three hours a week. Each week addresses a different topic.

	Receptive skills (reading & listening)	**Productive skills** (writing & speaking)	**Language work** (grammar & vocabulary)	**Review activities**
Week 1 Topic: ———				
Week 2 Topic: ———				

How could you fill in the grid?

- First decide on what the **main topic** will be for the week (for example *health, travel, education, lifestyles*, etc). If you are using a coursebook, then you can add the coursebook unit number and topic (eg Unit 5 – *Travel*).
- Then add which **skills** you will be covering in each week (*reading, writing*, etc). Add the coursebook page reference if relevant, or the material you will use (eg Listening – *travel podcasts*; Reading – *travel blogs*) in the appropriate column.
- For each skill and activity, think about whether it will involve **individual work**, **pair work**, or **group work**. Note this under each skill and activity. Note down under each section how long it will take.

You should now have a nicely balanced plan that could be offered entirely f2f. That's fine, but we want to offer our learners some online work. This work can be **synchronous** (learners and teacher are online at the same time) or **asynchronous** (learners and teacher do the online work at different times). Asynchronous work online is often the preferred mode of study for teachers and learners as it is more flexible. However, there are times when synchronous activities (eg chats, video-conferences) can be very helpful to build or reinforce group dynamics, or to practise speaking.

Asynchronous work online is more flexible. Synchronous activities can be very helpful to build group dynamics.

Options

Now let us imagine a few online learning scenarios for our example language course – where the learners spend three hours a week learning English. We provide four different online learning options for our group.

A Mainly face-to-face

Our first option – and the logical entry point for teachers who may be trying out online teaching for the first time and who may find it not only more comfortable, but also wiser, to begin here. This is probably one of the most common models of blended learning, and a good way to start introducing an online component to your learners, too.

In this option, our learners meet 70% face-to-face, while 30% of the course is carried out online. For our group of learners, this could involve the following:

- Meeting f2f twice a week for an hour
- Carrying out one hour of weekly coursework online

Below is our plan for the first two weeks of the course:

	f2f 70%			online 30%
	Receptive skills (reading & listening	**Productive skills** (writing & speaking)	**Language work** (grammar & vocabulary)	**Review activities**
Week 1 **Topic:** Hellos	Getting to know the VLE 'Me, myself and I' online activity [writing & reading] [individual] **1 hour online**	Course introductions Coursebook work [speaking] [groups, pairs] **1 hour f2f**	Coursebook work [grammar & vocab] [groups, pairs, individual] **1 hour f2f**	
Week 2 **Topic:** Travel	Read travel blogs Online podcasts on travel theme [reading & listening] [individual] **1 hour online**	Coursebook work [speaking & writing] [groups, pairs] **1 hour f2f**	Coursebook work [grammar & vocab] [pairs, individual] **40 m f2f**	Review of Week 1 **20 m f2f**

As you can see, we have gone through our f2f plan, and added what we will offer the learners f2f and what we will offer our group online.

As only 30% of the course content is delivered online, we have based the plan on the coursebook for f2f sessions and, for the online part, chosen online activities to supplement and complement the f2f classes.

- For the first two weeks, the online activities we choose focus mainly on the receptive skills, and we use internet-based materials which reinforce themes from the coursebook and which are continued in the f2f classes.
- As the course progresses, we can start to integrate more interactive online activities for the 30% online part of the course, covering the other skills (and possibly chosen from Part B of this book).

In our plan above, you will see that we have included fewer speaking online activities, as we will have plenty of time in f2f classes to give our learners speaking practice.

B Half-and-half

Now let us take our same group of learners, who study English for three hours a week. This time, let's imagine that we want to offer them the chance to complete 50% of their course f2f, and the other 50% online.

- The f2f meetings could take place regularly during the course (say once a week).
- Alternatively, they could take place at the beginning and/or end of the course.

You need to ensure the following:

- A balance of communicative skills and language work is achieved online.
- Opportunities for online group and pair work are also created.

You will probably include fewer group and individual speaking online activities, as you will have time in the f2f classes to deal with these.

Here is the plan for the first two weeks of coursework:

f2f			online
50%			50%

	Receptive skills (reading & listening)	**Productive skills** (writing & speaking)	**Language work** (grammar & vocabulary)	**Review activities**
Week 1 **Topic:** Hellos	Getting to know the VLE 'Me, myself and I' online activity [writing & reading] [individual] **1 hour online asynchronous**	'Blog diary' activity [writing] [individual] **30 m online asynchronous**	Course introductions Coursebook work [speaking, vocab, language work, listening] [groups, pairs, individual] **1½ hours f2f**	
Week 2 **Topic:** Travel	Reading travel blogs Online podcasts on travel theme [reading & listening] [individual] **1 hour online asynchronous**		Coursebook work [vocab, lang work & speaking] [pairs, groups] **1½ hours f2f**	'My window, my world' activity [writing & reading] [groups, individual] **30 m online asynchronous**

As in Option A, the topics for each week are taken from the coursebook.

- For the online component, we are integrating online activities from Part B of this book – and we are choosing topics for these online activities which reflect and reinforce topics from the f2f classes.
- The Week 2 topic is Travel, so the Week 2 podcast listening task asks learners to listen to someone talking on a similar topic, for example a learner living in an English-speaking country.

Basically, in Option B, we simply have more *online* activities integrated into our course plan than in Option A.

C Mainly online

Now let us look again at our same group of learners. This time, imagine that they meet infrequently f2f, and most of the coursework (80%) is carried out online. F2f meetings may take place at regular, although infrequent, intervals throughout the course (say once a month for two hours) and/or at the very beginning or end of the course.

Most of our course takes place online, so we need to ensure a balance of communicative skills and language work online, with plenty of opportunities for group and pair work online too.

- We will probably spend most of our f2f classes on speaking activities, as these are the most difficult to deliver effectively online.
- We will still make sure that the online part of the course includes regular group and individual speaking activities too, so that the online part of the course does not become too text-based.

Here is a plan for our first two weeks' work:

f2f			**online**	
20%			80%	

	Receptive skills (reading & listening)	Productive skills (writing & speaking)	Language work (grammar & vocabulary)	Review activities
Week 1 **Topic:** Hellos	Getting to know the VLE 'Me, myself and I' online activity [writing & reading] [individual] **1 hour online asynchronous**	'Blog diary' activity [writing] [individual] **1 hour online asynchronous**	'Name three …' activity 'Ready, steady, write!' activity [vocab] [groups] **1 hour online text chat synchronous**	
Week 2 **Topic:** Travel	Online podcasts on travel theme [listening] [individual] **30 m online asynchronous**	'Round the world' activity [speaking] [groups] **30 m online asynchronous**	'Wiki city' activity [writing & lang work] [pairs, groups] **1 hour online asynchronous**	Meet the group **1 hour first f2f session**

You can slot online coursebook-based activities into the grid if your learners each have their own copy of the book at home:

- Some of the reading activities could be coursebook readings, rather than online reading materials.
- We need to be careful that not all online work is coursebook-based, however, as we may then be in danger of making the online part of the course simply self-study, with no interaction taking place between learners online.

All of the online activities in the grid (and in Part B) encourage learners to *interact* online, and to use web-based materials and sites.

D Fully online

Finally, we will imagine that our learners are going to take their language course completely online and never meet f2f. In this scenario, we may well have learners in the group who are living in different countries, or we may even be teaching one-to-one.

Even though *all* of our coursework is carried out online, we still need to ensure:

- A balance of communicative skills and language work
- Plenty of opportunities for group and pair work, including regular online group and individual speaking activities

Here is our plan for the first two weeks' work, all of which will take place online:

online

100%

	Receptive skills (reading & listening)	**Productive skills** (writing & speaking)	**Language work** (grammar & vocabulary)	**Review activities**
Week 1 **Topic:** Hellos	Getting to know the VLE 'Me, myself and I' online activity *[writing & reading]* *[individual]* **1 hour online asynchronous**	'Blog diary' activity *[writing]* *[individual]* **1 hour online asynchronous**	'Name three …' activity 'Ready, steady, write!' activity' *[vocab]* *[groups]* **1 hour online text chat synchronous**	
Week 2 **Topic:** Travel	Online podcasts on travel theme *[listening]* *[individual]* **1 hour online asynchronous**	'Round the world' activity *[speaking]* *[groups]* **30 m online asynchronous**	'Wiki city' activity *[writing & lang work]* *[pairs, groups]* **1 hour online asynchronous**	'My window, my world' activity *[writing & reading]* *[groups, individual]* **30 m online asynchronous**

You will see that we have a good range of synchronous and asynchronous activities in the plan, and that we include a variety of online individual, pair and group work. It is important to make sure that this variety continues *throughout* the fully online course.

Online tools

The first decision to make at this stage is whether you want to use a set of tools which are all in one 'place' (such as a VLE – see below) to deliver your online course content, or whether you will use a variety of *separate* tools, such as email, text and voice chat programs, etc.

A Virtual Learning Environment (VLE) is an online platform which is accessible to learners, and in which course resources (such as documents, video, audio, etc) can be stored.

- Learners can interact via forums, chatrooms and learning journals, do assignments, quizzes or polls, and use tools such as wikis and blogs.
- Teachers can keep learners' grades in a VLE, and track progress and participation.

One of the biggest advantages of using a VLE for online course delivery, rather than a collection of disparate online tools, is that everything is in one place, and learners' work,

The first decision to make is whether you want to use a set of tools that are all in one 'place'.

It is easier to build a sense of online community among learners in a VLE, than by, say, email.

grades and contributions can be easily monitored. Being in one place (in this case, in one website!) it is also easier to build a sense of online community among learners in a VLE than by, say, email.

Some of the best-known VLEs are Blackboard/WebCT, First Class, Moodle and Sakai. Most have features in common; however, some VLEs are currently 'open source' and therefore free (Moodle; Sakai), while others are not free and can require substantial investment (Blackboard/WebCT and First Class). This is often a major consideration for educators, especially those that do not have institutional funding.

The other option is to use a number of *separate* tools to deliver the online part of your course. Communication can take place mainly by email, for example, and in online forums stored on separate web pages. Individual text and voice chat programs can be chosen for specific online activities. The advantage of using separate tools is that most of them are easy to use and teachers don't need much training to use the most basic of these.

Our own view is that a VLE provides a wealth of communicative tools in one place and is preferable to the separate tools approach for the reasons outlined.

These considerations are worth investigating as one of your first priorities.

- We would definitely recommend a VLE for courses which have a high percentage of online delivery – those courses described in Options B and C (as well as D!).
- We would also recommend for the teacher planning to use a VLE to receive adequate training, ensuring that all the tools are used effectively and appropriately.

We have included these considerations at this point because they are well worth considering – and investigating – as one of your first priorities.

Online teaching

Careful and thorough course planning and design is, therefore, one important aspect of offering online learning. Another is ensuring that you have the requisite technical and online tutor skills to deliver the course effectively and to support your learners online.

Here is a checklist of useful tips, or things to keep in mind, to help you run an effective online course.

- Get yourself up to speed with the tools you plan to use for online delivery. If you are familiar and confident with the tools yourself, you will be better able to help your learners. Almost all the free internet-based tools we look at in Part B of this book have tutorials and FAQs for the first-time user. Another good idea is to search a site like YouTube for video tutorials on how to use a tool – you will almost always find something to help you.
- Be prepared to offer your learners general technical help at times. Imagine you schedule an audio chat, but some of your learners are having problems with their microphones not working – some basic technical knowledge will help you deal with this on the spot. Having access to an IT support department that can offer fast and effective troubleshooting advice to learners would be ideal, but many teachers simply don't have this luxury. The good news is that you can learn to do many basic technical things by using computers yourself.

Communicating online is different to communicating f2f.

- Remember that communicating online is different to communicating f2f. For a start, there are none of the paralinguistic features such as gesture and facial expression to help communication, nor intonation patterns (if the communication is in writing) to help convey the tone of a message. Emails, postings and any form of online communication need to be polite, clear and unambiguous. Observe 'netiquette' and ensure that your learners do the same.
- Offer constant encouragement. This is important, especially if your course has a high percentage of online work – encouraging and motivating your learners is a key online tutor skill. Give individual feedback, celebrate individual and group achievements.

- Provide plenty of opportunities for socialisation at the beginning of the course, to help the group to gel – again, this is especially important if the course has a high percentage of online work. It is obviously less important if the group meets face-to-face at the very beginning of the course, and/or regularly throughout.
- Provide plenty of interactive online group and pair work throughout the course.
- Provide a space for the learners to express any concerns or worries to you online, eg via online office hours, email or private learning journals. And address these concerns if and when they arise.
- Take an online course *yourself* – this is an extremely effective way of gaining insights into how it feels to study online. You could take an online course in an area of interest to you, not necessarily learning a language.
- Consider training. Although good online tutoring is often a matter of common sense and being prepared to invest plenty of time, you may also want to look into training in online tutoring/e-moderation skills, or taking part in online conferences.

In Part C of *Teaching Online*, we shall be looking at ways of helping you to develop professionally and personally as online teachers.

Good online tutoring is often a matter of common sense and being prepared to invest plenty of time.

Overall

At the beginning of these pages, we saw how online teaching may be perceived as an ordeal or an opportunity by teachers. We have seen that, with the right preparation, teachers can experience an online teaching context as an opportunity, as a new challenge to be enjoyed. A good approach for the teacher wanting to introduce an online element into their teaching is to start small, by offering as little as 10 percent to 30 percent of a course online.

Planning online coursework is not dissimilar to planning face-to-face coursework – the same principles of balance and variety apply. Indeed, with a blended course, the best way to start is with your f2f course plan – your objectives. You can then more easily identify which elements can best be offered online.

The time has come to look in more detail at the tools that you will have the possibility of using.

Now that we have considered both the advantages and disadvantages of online teaching and have analysed how to introduce an online element into your courses – and before we begin implementing the activities and suggestions included in Part B – the time has come to look in more detail at the tools that you will have the possibility of using when you start *Teaching Online*. We have already presented on page 6 the hardware you will need.

> **Hardware** – the actual computer or microphone or screen

You will also need software – and to be very much aware of a third 'tool' that is perhaps often neglected, but the importance of which is absolutely fundamental, especially in pedagogical situations: 'liveware'.

> **Software** – programs that tell the computer what to do
>
> **Liveware** – the human factor

Software

One of the first things you will need to decide is where you will keep your online course content:

- Where will you give your learners instructions for tasks and add documents, audio files or videos?
- Where will your learners interact online, using text, audio or video?
- Where will you keep grades or provide feedback on their work?

We suggest that you set up a dedicated space, or course site, online. Think of this as a central hub where learners and teachers can meet and/or exchange information online. Here are some of the things that you can do in a course site:

Teachers	Learners
Give instructions for tasks	Find instructions for tasks
Read students' work	Post answers to tasks
Give feedback on work/assignments	Read feedback on individual and group work/assignments
Discuss issues with learners	Discuss issues with learners and teacher
Pick up messages from learners	Pick up messages from teacher
Leave messages for learners	Leave messages for teacher or other learners
Leave a list of useful links	Find useful links
Leave audio and video files	Listen to audio and watch video
Hold text and video chats	Attend text and video chat with teacher and learners
Create quizzes and polls	Do quizzes and polls
Manage student grades	Access grades privately

What exactly does a course site consist of? If you work in a large school or institution – such as a university – there may already be an official online space, such as a Virtual Learning Environment, for you to use. If you are starting a course from scratch and work on your own, you may not have access to an institutional VLE and will have to create a course site yourself. The good news is that nowadays this is much easier than before, and it's free. The tools we list below can each serve as a course site and the ones we recommend as 'Our favourites' are free at the time of writing.

We start with VLEs, then take a look at social networking sites, then at wikis, and finally at online discussion groups. You could run your online course using any of these tools as a central hub or course site. Bear in mind:

- VLEs offer the most complete solution for online courses, as they can do *all* of the things we outlined above.
- Some social networking sites can do *most* of the things outlined, wikis can do *many*, and online discussion groups can do *some* of the things we mentioned.

So when deciding which tool to use as your course site, your order of preference should be: a VLE – a social networking site – a wiki – and, your final choice, an online discussion group.

For each tool we provide a suggested 'Search term', so that you can look for other tools besides those that we recommend. This is worth doing as new tools are appearing all the time. All the tools we suggest are current at the time of writing.

Our favourites
Over the next seven pages, we will be listing in this column some of our favourite course site tools and activity tools. They are obviously not the only ones, but we are comfortable in recommending them.

Course site tools

◼ VLEs

Drupal
http://drupal.org
Elgg
http://elgg.org
Moodle
http://moodle.com

What they do ... VLE is short for 'Virtual Learning Environment'. VLEs are online course management systems designed for teachers to run online courses. They usually include course content, communication tools (eg forums, chat, wikis, blogs), grading tools, learner tracking, grouping facilities and control over who can access the course. Some VLEs are free (see our list of favourites on the left).

What you do ... For some VLEs, you will need a place to 'host' it. This could be a school server, or a private server. VLEs are tools with many different functions, so they take time to prepare and set up. You will probably need help and training for this. Once you have your VLE set up and some course content added, you can enrol your learners – and begin your course.

Search term ... 'virtual learning environment'

◼ Social networking sites

SocialGO
http://www.socialgo.com
WackWall
http://wackwall.com
Grouply
http://www.grouply.com

What they do ... Social networking sites are websites that allow members to create their own profile page and link to other members in the site. The most famous examples are MySpace and Facebook. However, these are less suited for education. Best for your online course site are the ones we recommend opposite. Most will have a discussion area and the possibility for members to upload photos, documents and videos.

What you do ... First you need to sign up to a social networking site. Then create your network. You can usually customise the appearance of your network. Check the site instructions on what to do. Invite your learners to your network. Each learner will be assigned a page, where they can upload a photo and complete personal information about themselves.

Search term ... 'create social network'

◼ Wikis

Google Sites
http://sites.google.com
PBworks
http://pbworks.com
Wetpaint
http://www.wetpaint.com
Wikispaces
http://www.wikispaces.com

What they do ... Wikis consist of a series of collaborative web pages to which anyone with permission can contribute. You can add text, images, video and audio to wikis. You can also upload documents.

What you do ... First you need to sign up to a wiki site. Then create your wiki. This is usually as easy as clicking on a few buttons. Check the site instructions on what to do. Once you have created a wiki, you can invite your learners to join. Many wikis are 'password protected' – this means that only users with the password can make changes to the content.

Changes to wiki web pages are automatically saved, and can be retrieved and restored. So even if someone deletes the content of an entire wiki page by mistake, it's possible to go back and restore it!

Search term ... 'create wiki'

◼ Discussion groups

Google Groups
http://groups.google.com
Nicenet
http://www.nicenet.org
Yahoo Groups
http://groups.yahoo.com

What they do ... Online discussion groups are electronic lists in which list members communicate by email. Participants can exchange email messages and can also usually upload documents, images or video to a shared web page.

What you do ... First you need to sign up to a discussion group site. Then create your group. Almost all discussion lists can be made private, so that members need a password to join, or to access files or members' names. Someone usually starts a discussion topic, to which other people respond. Messages are stored on the discussion group web page, and are sent to members by email.

Search term ... 'online discussion group tool'

Activity tools

Many of the tools in Part B are examples of so-called 'Web 2.0' tools. This simply means that they are tools that allow users to contribute materials easily. Think of the difference between a 'static' website – to which the casual visitor or user cannot contribute – and a wiki, which anybody with permission can contribute to. A wiki is an example of a Web 2.0 tool.

Another feature of Web 2.0 tools is that they have multi-functionality. To take our example:

- A wiki does not have to consist only of text.
- It can include videos, audio, a calendar, embedded documents, an area for learners to upload assignments, automatic translation or glossary tools, a guest map – to name a few of the extras you can integrate.

So when we suggest that you do an activity with your learners using text chat, you probably use a tool that combines text chat with audio and/or video-conferencing capabilities, as well as a shared whiteboard!

In this section, we suggest specific examples of tools with their web addresses, and we have tried to choose tools which we think are here to stay. However, be aware that Web 2.0 tools appear and disappear, and new applications and tools are constantly appearing. We hope that by providing you with some key search terms for each tool, we will help you find new ones, too – tools which don't yet exist at the time of writing.

Once you have your course online (or part of your course, if you doing a blended option) you may still wish to use other web-based tools to do various activities. Some of these may already exist in your course site, especially if you are using a VLE, but for others you will merely have to send your learners the link for them to use it. Some of these tools require users to register. The information they require is minimum.

- We advise you to create a separate email address to coordinate everything relating to your course, and register for any extra sites using that address.
- It's also a good idea to use the *same* username and password for your course-related registrations (easier to remember!) or to keep a safe record of all your usernames and passwords.

One of the most common problems that we see teachers have is registering for a new site, then forgetting the email they used to register and their username and password!

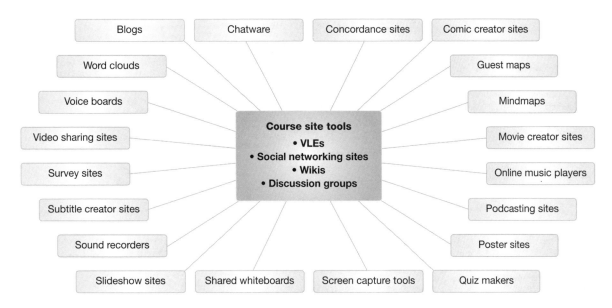

🔲 Blogs

Blog.com
http://blog.com

Blogger
http://www.blogger.com

LiveJournal
http://www.livejournal.com

Wordpress
http://wordpress.org

What they do ... Blogs are online journals or diaries. They consist of a series of 'posts', which appear on a web page in reverse chronological order (so the latest post appears at the top of the page). Blogs can be on any topic. Blogs used in education are called 'edublogs'.

What you do ... First you need to sign up for a blog on the homepage. Once you have created your blog, you need to decide whether you want to use it as a class, learner or teacher blog. A class blog is a single blog set up by the teacher, to which all the learners contribute. A learner blog is set up and contributed to by an individual learner – in other words, each learner has their own separate learner blog. A teacher blog belongs to the teacher alone.

Search term ... 'create blog'

🔲 Chatware

Active Worlds
http://www.activeworlds.com
Second Life
http://www.secondlife.com

Google Talk
http://www.google.com/talk
MSN Messenger
http://messenger.live.com
Skype
http://www.skype.com

3
Dimdim
http://www.dimdim.com
WiZiQ
http://www.wiziq.com

What it does ... Chatware is software for communicating in real-time over the internet. Chatware includes *text* chat, *voice* chat (like the telephone) and *video* chat (or video-conferencing). More sophisticated forms of chatware include 3D virtual worlds [1]. The more sophisticated the chatware, the better your internet connection needs to be. Very simple chatware (such as text chat, also called 'instant messaging') can take place on low bandwidth or dial-up connections without too much trouble. High-end chatware, such as video-conferencing or virtual worlds, needs a fast broadband connection to work well, as well as a computer with a video graphics card (these come installed with all modern computers).

The kind of chatware you choose will depend on the aim of the activity (several of the activities in Part B suggest using text chat, which can be excellent for language practice) and your own and your learners' hardware and internet connections.

What you do ... You need to download some chatware onto your computer and, to use it with others, *they* need to have the same chatware on *their* computer [2]. However, some chatware is web-based and allows you to create a video-conference online without any downloading [3]. Once you've set up and logged into a video-conference with a username, you can invite others to join you by sending them a web link, which will take them to the video-conference. Many video-conferencing tools will also include a shared whiteboard and the option of browsing a web page together. You need a headset to take part in voice chat, and a headset and webcam for video-conferencing.

Search term ... 'online chat tool' or 'online video conference tool' or 'virtual world'

🔲 Concordance sites

British National Corpus
http://www.natcorp.ox.ac.uk
Compleat Lexical Tutor
http://www.lextutor.ca
Cobuild Concordance and Collocations Sampler
http://www.collins.co.uk/Corpus/CorpusSearch.aspx

What they do ... Concordance sites allow you to search large collections of spoken or written text ('corpora') to see how words are used in context. The results of your search are displayed as a 'concordance' – in lines. Here is a concordance for the word 'home':

What you do ... Go to a concordance site, type in the word you want to research (eg 'home') and the results will be displayed in concordance lines. You can usually select which lines to extract and redisplay at this stage, to limit your examples. Take a screenshot (google 'how to take a screenshot' if you are unsure how) and add your concordance to a word-processing document, or print it out for your learners.

Search term ... 'concordance software'

Screenshot example taken from:
http://www.lextutor.ca

Comic creator sites

MakeBeliefs Comix
http://www.makebeliefscomix.com/
ToonDoo
http://www.toondoo.com
Comicbrush
http://www.comicbrush.com/

What they do ... Comic creator sites allow you to create strip cartoons or comics.

What you do ... Go to your chosen comic site, and create a comic. Not all sites require you to sign up first. These sites usually work on a template system. First you choose your characters, then you type what your characters say in speech bubbles. You can choose several frames for your comic, to create a short story or situation. Or you can choose just one frame. Some sites let you use photos, and some allow you to draw your own.

Search term ... 'create comics'

Guest maps

Bravenet
http://www.bravenet.com/
webtools/guestmap
ClustrMaps
http://www.clustrmaps.com
MyGuestmap
http://www.mapservices.org

What they do ... Guest map tools allow viewers or members to add information to a world map, and for others to see that information.

What you do ... You have to register in the site to create a guest map. Once you have an account, you can start adding information and share the link to your map with others. Other people usually do not need to register to add information to the world map.

Search term ... 'create guest map'

Mindmaps

Lovely Charts
http://www.lovelycharts.com
Text2Mindmap
http://www.text2mindmap.com
XMind
http://www.xmind.net

What they do ... Mindmapping tools enable you to create visual mindmaps or graphic organisers.

What you do ... Go to the mindmapping tool site of your choice. In some cases, you need to download and install the mindmapping program, but others are web-based so require no downloading. Enter the words you want to include in your mindmap and the groups you want them to be in, and the program will convert them into a mindmap. Many of these programs allow you to copy and download the completed mindmap.

Search term ... 'mindmapping software'

Movie creator sites

Dvolver
http://www.dvolver.com
Voki
http://www.voki.com
Xtranormal
http://www.xtranormal.com

What they do ... Movie creator sites enable you to create animated movies with text and/or audio, and to share them with other people online.

What you do ... Many movie creator sites are free to use, although you may have to register to save your movie. They follow a template system: you choose the background, then the characters and their clothing; you decide what the characters say, etc. Some movie sites work with captions (you read what the movie characters say via little voice bubbles) while others have text-to-voice software which allows the animated characters to speak.

Search term ... 'make movies online'

Online music players

Deezer
http://www.deezer.com
Grooveshark
http://listen.grooveshark.com
Spotify
http://www.spotify.com

What they do ... Online music players are programs that let you choose and listen to music online.

What you do ... You choose songs you want to hear from music libraries online. You can create playlists and share them with other people. However, you cannot download the songs from the internet onto your computer. Many online music players are free; some (eg Spotify) have a monthly fee – but also have a much bigger library of songs to choose from.

Search term ... 'online music player'

Podcasting sites

PodBean
http://www.podbean.com/
PodOmatic
http://www.podomatic.com
VoiceThread
http://voicethread.com

What they do ... Podcasting sites allow you to record and share media files (usually audio, but also video – these are known as 'vodcasts' or 'video podcasts'). Your podcast 'episodes' (recordings) then appear on a web page, in reverse chronological order (with the latest at the top of the page). You can also add text and pictures to your podcast episodes.

What you do ... You need first to sign up for an account in your chosen podcasting site. Record your audio in the site itself, or upload audio from your computer, as a series of individual episodes. You can include pictures and text with each episode. Other people can listen to your podcast in the site itself, and leave comments (if you enable this). Or they can subscribe to your podcast site and automatically receive new episodes to their computer. You can make your podcasts public or private. You will need a headset or microphone to create your podcasts.

Search term ... 'create podcast'

Poster sites

Glogster
http://www.glogster.com
Museum Box
http://museumbox.e2bn.org
Wallwisher
http://www.wallwisher.com

What they do ... Poster sites allow you to make posters online. Because they are web-based, you can add a range of media to your poster, such as text, images, audio and video. This makes for a rich and engaging multimedia experience when viewing the poster online.

What you do ... Most poster sites require you to create a user account. Once you have this, you create a poster and add text, images, audio and/or video. You can add your own digital images and record your own audio or video, or use pre-recorded audio or video (such as a song or music video) in your online poster. The overall effect is of a collage. The poster has a unique web address, and is viewed online. If the poster includes multimedia, you click on the audio or video to hear or view it.

Search term ... 'create online poster'

Quiz makers (or Authoring tools)

Hot Potatoes
http://hotpot.uvic.ca
MyStudiyo
http://www.mystudiyo.com
Puzzlemaker
http://puzzlemaker.
discoveryeducation.com
ProProfs
http://www.proprofs.com
Quizlet
http://quizlet.com

What they do ... Quiz makers allow you to make quizzes that your students can then do online. You can usually choose from a range of question types to create your quiz, including multiple-choice, 'yes/no' questions, cloze tests and gap fills. Some sites allow you to create crosswords or flashcards.

What you do ... Some quiz makers are web-based, so you simply type in your questions online. Others (such as Hot Potatoes) require you to download and install a program on your computer to create your quiz, which you can then upload to the internet for your learners to access. They do the quiz and are given a grade. The quiz is automatically graded, but when you type in your quiz questions in some quiz makers you can also type in feedback for each question, such as 'Incorrect. You need to review the simple past!' or 'Well done!'.

Search term ... 'create online quiz'

Screen capture tools

CamStudio
http://camstudio.org
Jing
http://www.jingproject.com
Screencast
http://www.screencast.com

What they do ... Screen capture software can record what you show on your screen, to make a video for others to watch. You can provide an audio commentary as you record things on your computer screen, and this will also be heard in the recorded video.

What you do ... Once you have downloaded the software, you select the part of the screen you wish to record. You can then speak into a microphone while you are working on the screen, and the software will record your voice and what you see on the screen. You can share this video with others. You will need a microphone to record yourself while capturing what's on your screen.

Search term ... 'screen capture software'

■ Shared whiteboards

What they do ... Shared whiteboards are tools on which teacher and learners can work together in real-time on a virtual whiteboard.

What you do ... Many shared whiteboards come with a 'text chat' function or as part of a video-conferencing tool. On a shared whiteboard, you or your learners can write, type or draw, and the others will see what you are doing in real-time. You can also often upload images, documents or PowerPoint slides to a shared whiteboard, for everyone to see.

Search term ... 'online shared whiteboard'

■ Slideshow sites

What they do ... Slideshow sites enable you to upload and share PowerPoint presentations (or other slide presentations) online.

What you do ... You have to register with your chosen slideshow site to create an online slideshow. Once you have an account, you can simply upload your presentation and send a link for others to see it online. Presentations can be PowerPoint presentations or a series of photos. Some slideshow sites allow you to make slides from word-processed documents, and to add text and/or audio commentary to your slideshow.

Search term ... 'create slideshow'

■ Sound recorders

What they do ... Sound recorders enable you to record yourself directly via your computer.

What you do ... Your PC or Mac computer software comes with a sound recorder included. This is simply a piece of software that allows you to record yourself with a microphone, and to save the audio file to your computer. It has clear and easy-to-use Record, Stop, Pause and Play buttons. You can then send the audio file to others, or upload it to a forum, blog, wiki or VLE.

Search term ... [You need to look in your computer programs for the sound recorder.]

■ Subtitle creator sites

What they do ... Subtitle creator sites let you add your own subtitles to an existing video clip.

What you do ... Some subtitle sites work with a selection of foreign film clips which you can subtitle (these are sites meant for fun, as the film clips are from very obscure or strange films). Other sites allow you to input any video file from a site such as YouTube and subtitle that.

Search term ... 'online subtitle creator'

■ Survey (or Questionnaire) sites

What they do ... Online survey sites allow you to make surveys, polls or questionnaires that others can complete online. These surveys can be public (viewable by everyone on the internet) or private (you set a password which your learners enter when they visit the survey site). Most survey sites will also have a 'results' function, showing you the results of your survey in percentages and graphs.

What you do ... You have to register in your chosen survey site to create a survey. There is usually a list of possible question types (multiple-choice, open-answer, etc) for you to choose from, and you can include different kinds of question types in the same survey. Create your survey, and then send the link to your learners for them to complete.

Search term ... 'create online survey'

Video sharing sites

blipTV
http://blip.tv
TeacherTube
http://www.teachertube.com
YouTube
http://www.youtube.com

What they do ... Video sharing sites allow you to upload and share videos.

What you do ... You can record a video with your webcam or digital camera, then upload it to the video sharing site. Other people can watch your video in the site. You can also often embed your video from a video sharing site into other sites (eg into your blog or wiki). You can make your video public (so that anyone can view it) or private (so that only those with the web address can view it).

Search term ... 'video sharing site'

Voice boards

Snapvine
http://www.snapvine.com
Utterli
http://www.utterli.com
Voxopop
http://www.voxopop.com

What they do ... Voice boards allow you to record yourself and add your audio file to a web page. Voice boards are to audio what forums are to written text – message boards on which to leave audio comments.

What you do ... You subscribe to your chosen voice board site, create your profile and then you can start recording audio messages in the site itself. You need a microphone or headset to do this. You can create closed groups for your messages – the people you invite to your group (eg your learners) can then listen to your audio comments and leave audio and/or text replies. In this way, a 'threaded' discussion in audio can be built up on a single web page. Some voice boards (eg Snapvine) function more as audio blogs.

Search term ... 'voice message board'

Word clouds

Tagxedo
http://www.tagxedo.com
TagCrowd
http://tagcrowd.com
Wordle
http://www.wordle.net

What they do ... Word cloud sites create word clouds – visual depictions of key words in an attractive format. The most frequent words from a text are often represented in bigger type.

What you do ... Just enter the words you want to use in your chosen word cloud site and the tool will create the word cloud. Most word cloud sites don't require you to register. You can type in a list of words, or copy in a short text and the site will choose the key words from the text. The results are then presented in a cloud. You can usually change the colours and fonts of the words. You can save your cloud as a web page, and/or print it out.

Search term ... 'word cloud generator'

Liveware

Teaching online is more than tackling the technology. It is still teaching. No matter how smooth your technical delivery, you are still running language courses.

The rules of the online game are different to the rules of teaching face-to-face in some ways, but similar in others. There are many things you already do as a teacher that you will do in your online teaching.

- When you start a real-time online class using text chat or video-conferencing, you will want to welcome your learners, just as you do in the f2f classroom.
- When your learners have produced work individually or collaboratively, you will want to congratulate and praise their achievements, just as you do in the f2f classroom.

You will want to ensure a good group dynamic during the course, and that your learners know how and where to interact effectively and courteously online. You will want to celebrate achievements with the group, and to make sure the learners meet the course objectives and deadlines that you establish. The question is *how* to do this online.

In this section we look at the basic behaviours that we regularly carry out online, as teachers and learners, and give you some advice about how to do this most effectively.

Meeting and greeting

We meet and greet our learners in two senses on an online course. First, if the course is starting online we need to set up 'getting to know you' activities to ensure that the group gels well and is able to work together effectively online for the duration of the course. We explore meeting and greeting (or online 'socialising') activities in detail in Chapter 1.

Also, you will probably want to run real-time (or 'synchronous') sessions with your learners at various points in your course. These will typically last between 45 and 60 minutes. This type of activity requires you to meet and greet your learners much as you would do in a 'real' class – but online. How? Here are some suggestions:

Greet the learners as they arrive in the online chatroom. Greet them by name, and engage in some chit-chat while you wait for the rest of the group to arrive.

- If your learners are in different places, you can ask them what the weather is like, or what time it is, or what they were doing before the chat started. And you can ask them how the course is going.
- If learners arrive in the chatroom late, you can simply put your greeting in brackets in the text chat window so that it comes across as an 'aside' – *[Hi Ivan, we've just started.]* – and doesn't interrupt the flow of conversation.

Once all your learners are in the chatroom, you can get everyone's attention by asking if they are ready to start. Wait for everyone to type 'yes' (or to say yes, if you are using audio). Then you can draw their attention to the agenda for your chat, and start your chat warmer activity.

These suggestions may sound obvious, but it´s important to prepare and plan a real-time chat beforehand. Your learners should be aware there is an agenda or outcome to their chat, whether it is a text chat or involves audio or video-conferencing. Real-time chat text, especially, has a tendency to get 'messy', with overlapping turns and interruptions as people type simultaneously.

- Give your learners clear guidelines for turn taking, for when and how to contribute in chats, as well as having a clear structure for the chat yourself.
- Keep in mind that the spontaneous nature of text chat, which reflects the cut and thrust of real-time conversation, is part of its appeal, and a certain amount of messiness and redundancy is inevitable.

Your chatware should record the interaction, and you should make sure it is made available to your learners afterwards. This is especially useful for learners who can't participate. The text chat script or video/audio recording can also form the basis for future language work.

Establishing objectives

Your course, whether partly or fully online, should have clear objectives. Some of these may relate to activities or projects carried out in your f2f sessions or to your online work, or to both. In setting tasks online, it's always a good idea to spell out the objective or aim in the task instructions. We recommend laying out your instructions following a simple clear template such as this:

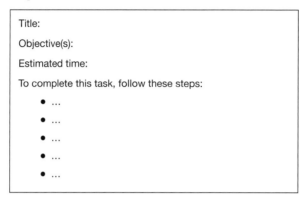

Title:

Objective(s):

Estimated time:

To complete this task, follow these steps:

- …
- …
- …
- …
- …

Instructions online need to be clearly staged so that learners are absolutely sure about what they need to do to complete a task successfully. Numbers, letters or bullet points for each task stage help break the content down. Adding an estimate for how long you think the task will take to complete is also helpful – we suggest using a time band, such as 10–15 or 30–45 minutes, rather than trying to calculate an exact time, which is notoriously difficult for online work!

Celebrating achievements

What about when objectives have been achieved? What do we do when our learners have successfully completed an online task or project? In the f2f classroom we give ongoing praise and feedback on completed tasks, with a quick comment such as 'Well done, Maria, that's great' while we are walking around the class monitoring work. Online, we need to be conscious of the extra importance of providing overt feedback and praise, and of celebrating learners' achievements.

If you are using discussion forums on your course, you need to post regularly and in a timely fashion responding to your learners' work. Apart from individual postings which respond to individual learners' comments as an ongoing process, you can post summarising the things that have gone well with a task. Ensure your praise and/or feedback during a course is delivered via a mixture of public (eg a forum) and private (eg via email) channels.

- You can congratulate learners on what they have achieved, and highlight the objectives that have been met, and how.
- You can also point to areas that need more work, and provide further links or resources for weaker areas, but this always needs to be framed in positive comments on what has gone well overall.

Remember that, online, there are no gestures or smiles to soften your words, so you need to be liberal with praise and judicious with criticism, which must always be constructive. Remember, too, that celebrating achievements and objectives met does not only need to come from the teacher. Your learners can share their own insights from a task or project in a forum, blog or wiki. They can give positive feedback on their colleagues' work as well, in any of these tools.

Dealing with deadlines

Getting learners to meet deadlines online can be a challenge. We have found that it's helpful to have very clear, regular deadlines for tasks – weekly, or perhaps fortnightly. If *you* take these deadlines seriously, so will your learners. Here are some suggestions:

- Ensure that your learners are aware of the importance of deadlines – that they are aware of how to ask for deadline extensions and it is clear under what circumstances extensions will be granted.
- Be flexible with individual learners, depending on circumstances – but having a clear framework for deadlines and extensions *before you start* will encourage sticking to them.

Also, before the course starts, provide some tips about time management and online learning. You could set up a brief discussion in a forum, for example, in which the learners share tips on how they are going to manage their learning, including exactly when during each week they will be completing their online tasks and where they will be working from (home, office, internet café, etc).

- Tell your learners to let you and their colleagues know in advance if there are any periods of time in which they are going to be away and unable to participate in coursework. This way you can adjust pair and group work accordingly. You can also send a learner work in advance.
- Include a calendar on the front page – if you use a VLE or wiki for your course space – in which deadlines for assignments or projects are clearly marked.

You can also offer regular online office hours in which you are available in your text or video-conferencing chatroom, or on a platform like Skype. For example, tell your learners that they can contact you directly every Monday and Wednesday between 10am and 11am. If they are from different countries, ensure that your office hours cover a range of time zones.

Of course, even with the best-laid plans and guidelines in place, there will be times when your learners inevitably miss important deadlines, or don't complete work. Speaking individually to them about progress and work not completed is always best done face-to-face. However, if your course is fully online, you will need to contact and support the learner at a distance. We suggest first sending an individual email to check whether they have been away, or whether there is any other specific reason for non-completed work and missed deadlines. You can also arrange to have a telephone or online audio chat with the learner privately during your online office hours.

Being polite

As well as deciding *what* tools to use in your online course, you will need to keep in mind how your learners *use* these tools to communicate. In face-to-face classes, communication is enhanced through paralinguistic features, such as facial expression or gestures. Online, these features are missing, and it is sometimes difficult to know when a person is trying to be amusing, ironic or sarcastic. The written word online can easily be misconstrued. And this problem is compounded when learners are expressing themselves in a foreign language – a learner who tries to be brief and to the point may come across as abrupt and rude.

Happily, there are ways in which we can help our learners communicate online more effectively:

- Establish some 'ground rules' for working and communicating together in the first few days or weeks of your online course.
- Review some of the common rules of 'netiquette' (the conventions for communicating online), or encourage your learners to establish their own ground rules.

What are the most commonly accepted netiquette rules? We will finish with a list of recommendations which explore netiquette – the rules of courtesy that apply as much to you, the teacher, as to your learners.

Netiquette

- **Respect**

  Be respectful of others' opinions online, even if you disagree. There are several useful phrases you can give your learners to show polite disagreement: *'You make a good/interesting/relevant point, but I also think that …'* or *'Thank you for highlighting this important issue, but we mustn't forget that …'.*

- **Acknowledgement**

  Encourage your learners to acknowledge others' opinions and ideas. You can provide them with useful phrases to do this: *'Thanks for bringing this up, Miguel, this is a very interesting point'* or *'I really like your point about X'.*

- **Thinking before writing**

  Invite your learners to think carefully about their responses to their course colleagues' work before they post a response. Postings should always be supportive and, even if they disagree with the content of a post, they should try to emphasise at least one positive point and should always use polite language.

- **Humour**

  It can be very difficult to convey humour online, especially in a foreign language. Suggest that your learners use emoticons to show that they are not serious, for example by using a smiley face :-) or a wink icon ;-). However, not everyone likes emoticons – see the point below.

- **Emoticons**

  Although emoticons can be used to indicate humour, or a less serious statement, they should not be overused. To sensitise your learners to possible overuse, you could show them two short texts, one full of emoticons (inappropriate use) and the same text with just one or two – to illustrate appropriate use.

- **Capital letters**

  There is general agreement that using capital letters in online writing comes across as SHOUTING. Ask your learners not to use capital letters in their online writing. They can emphasise words by using bold or italics, or by placing stars on either side of the word to be emphasised, *like this*.

- **Acronyms**

  Acronyms, such as LOL for 'laugh out loud' or BTW for 'by the way', are fairly common in online forums and emails. If you think the use of acronyms is acceptable, we suggest that you ask your learners to explain what the acronyms stand for the first few times they use them. Not everybody is familiar with them or what they mean.

- **Texting language**

  Abbreviated forms, such as CU for 'see you' or L8R for 'later', are common in mobile phone texting, and can also be seen in some public online forums on the internet. Generally speaking, though, the use of abbreviated texting language would be considered unsuitable on a language learning course – unless you wanted to do a specific activity on these forms (which are useful in their own right). Especially pernicious is the use of a lowercase *'i'* instead of *'I'* – this is one texting form that you may want to ensure your language learners *don't* use online. It can often look like a mistake rather than the deliberate use of a texting form.

Teaching Online has so far examined the hardware, the software and, most importantly, the liveware – the human factor. Online teaching is as much about creating communication, rapport and interaction as classroom teaching is: we still have the teacher, the students, the language. The main difference is that these all-important human elements are mediated by machines. In this process of mediation there are, of course, some changes and adjustments. Talking face-to-face is not the same as talking via the telephone or via a webcam. But essentially, we are still talking about communication, and this is something that we all know is vital for learning a language.

Online teaching

All the activities presented in Part B are underpinned by the idea that communication and interaction are key for effective language teaching. Although we suggest a range of tools and sites for delivering the content of your course, we focus on activities that encourage learners to engage and interact *with* and *in* the language.

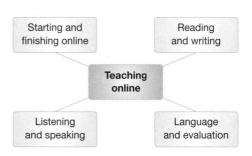

It is important never to lose sight of the liveware, and it is unlikely that computers will ever replace the teacher. Good online teaching needs effective human mediation – and this is provided by the teacher, not by automatic 'drag and drop' activities.

Online learning

There is a wealth of tools and sites available for English language learning. These range from 'static' sites which provide ready-made multimedia resources and lesson plans, to online tools which learners can use to create their own multimedia content and projects.

Our activities refer you to tools your learners can access both as *users* and as *creators* – and we suggest ways in which to encourage them to interact and communicate in English. We are not suggesting that you do *all* of these activities, nor that you do them in the order in which we present them. Depending on what your learners need, you can pick and choose as you please.

Note We list the tools you and your learners can use for each activity – in the order in which you will use them. And we use the generic term 'course site' to refer to any of the four main course site tools suggested on page 20 (VLE, discussion group, social networking site, wiki) through which you can package up and deliver your course content.

Chapter 1
The starting line

Activities

- Me, myself and I
- May I introduce myself?
- Hello, this is me
- My window, my world
- My precious …
- Slidesharing
- On the map
- Sounds of me
- Sounds of you
- What do you want?
- Things in common
- Find someone who …

Aim

These 'starting line' activities aim to provide you with a range of ways to get to know your learners online, and for them to get to know each other. If the learners start their course online, it is especially important that you include a range of these types of activities, so that a good group dynamic can be developed to support online work.

If you are teaching a course that is part online and part face-to-face (f2f), the course may start online. In this case, it is important to plan early activities around the learners getting to know each other and creating an online sense of 'community'. This means that when they do meet f2f later, the group will gel much quicker. In a 100% online course, it is vital that plenty of time is set aside for this initial stage of 'climate setting' or socialising.

Community

Creating a strong sense of online community in the group will help sustain your learners' motivation during the course, will make them feel supported by the teacher and by the other learners, and will ensure that they have a stronger sense of responsibility in group and pair work.

In courses where sufficient time has been set aside for online socialising activities, learners often report feeling a strong sense of accountability and responsibility in online activities. This feeling is only going to be possible if there is a strong sense of community.

Knowledge

Many learners today – especially the younger ones – will be familiar with blogs, social networking sites, wikis and a range of multimedia. However, before referring your learners to any of the web-based tools we suggest, you need to check that they do know how to use them. They will need to know how to register and create a user account to use some sites, as well as how to add their profiles and photos, etc.

If learners are doing these 'getting to know you' activities online before meeting f2f, you can point them to tutorials on the site itself – several of the sites and tools we recommend incorporate good video tutorials to help first-time users. Alternatively, you yourself could prepare a short guide with screenshots of the site, in Word or similar, to show them how to use it.

Correction

In the early stage of your online course, we recommend not correcting 'in public' everything a learner posts. Just as in a face-to-face 'getting to know you' activity we would not jump on a learner and correct them publicly, we should not do so online either.

The objective is for them to become comfortable with working online and to get to know each other. It may be worth stating this at the beginning of your course for those learners who always wish to have everything corrected. You can of course store the language the learners have produced in these early activities as diagnostic material to prepare future lessons. Learners can also be encouraged to revisit things they have posted, later in the course, to 'tidy up' their English.

Exposure

Some of the activities in this chapter ask learners to add information about themselves to public internet sites, such as social networking sites. You need to make it clear that anyone can read this information. By posting information about ourselves online, we are creating a 'digital footprint', and learners need be to fully aware of this fact. They need to add things to these sites that they are happy for anyone to read.

Some sites or tools (such as blogs and wikis) offer 'privacy settings', so you and your learners can decide exactly who has access to their information or work. If you are working online with young learners, you may decide *not* to use certain internet sites or tools if the privacy settings are not stringent enough.

Privacy

Privacy settings, such as those found on most blog, wiki or podcasting sites, will typically allow the following levels of access and control:

- Open to anyone to read and add comments
- Open to anyone to read and add comments, but the comments are 'moderated'
- Open to anyone to read, but only approved members can add comments
- Open only to approved members to read and add comments

Moderated comments are automatically sent to the owner of the blog, wiki or podcast for approval before publication.

Balance

It is worth discussing all of these options with your learners, to see which settings they are most comfortable with and what is most suitable in your teaching context. It is also worth keeping in mind that one of the advantages of using internet-based tools is that people from all over the world can in theory visit and comment on your learners' work; this sharing, and access to a worldwide audience, will be blocked if privacy settings are too stringent.

At the end of the day, it's a matter of balance – and discussing openly what is most appropriate for you and your learners.

Copyright

Several of the activities in this chapter also suggest that learners upload images to sites. Sometimes they will need to use images from the internet; this is fine, as long as copyright is respected. Tell your learners that they need to check that an image has a 'creative commons' copyright license – in which case, they may be able to use it freely.

Tell them to do a creative commons search for images, music, video, etc, by using the following search engine: http://search.creativecommons.org/. They then need to see exactly what conditions, if any, apply to using that work, by carefully reading the license.

Language

If your learners have a very low level of English, and the same first language, you may decide that some of these early activities can be carried out in their mother tongue. It is most important that they get to know each other as effectively as possible, especially if your course *starts* online. If using the mother tongue is going to help create a strong sense of online community, then it's worth letting the learners carry out at least some of these socialising activities in their first language.

Exactly how much L1 you allow will depend on your learners, their expectations, their age, etc. It is worth exploring the L1 option with them first, for example by carrying out a brief online survey of their opinions.

The starting line

In short, if your course is going to start out online or is offered in a blended model with a high proportion of work carried out online, then it is important that you spend time creating a strong sense of online community. We suggest the following:

- You start by introducing yourself online.
- Your learners share information about themselves via pictures, online maps and sounds.
- They can then get to know each other better in real-time text or video chats.

Our activities use a range of media, tools and skills. Some require learners to write, others to speak. Select any activities you wish, in the order you wish. Whichever ones you choose, perhaps include one or two that get the learners *speaking* online. And perhaps one or two that get them *writing*.

Me, myself and I

Introducing yourself online via text

Tools ▶ Course site

Technique

- Prepare a short profile about yourself, of 100–150 words. Include general information such as:
  - Your hobbies
  - Your job
  - Your studies
  - Your family
  - Where you live

  Include, too, several interesting or unusual things about yourself.

- Add this profile to your course site. Add a photo of yourself and/or your family.

- Ask your learners to read your profile.
  - They prepare a similar profile about themselves.
  - They add their profiles and photos to the course site.

- They visit each other's profiles and leave comments. Give them a task to complete while reading the profiles, with a series of questions like the ones in the box below.

Follow-up

You could refer to the information gleaned from the profiles in your first group online chat (see *What do you want?* on page 39). You could also create a quiz out of the information for when the group first meets f2f.

Comment

It is a good idea to ask your learners to add to their profiles not only general information, but some *unusual* information about themselves. This makes it a much more interesting read for their course colleagues!

- Who lives in the same town/region/country/ continent as you?
- Who has the same or similar hobbies as you?
- Whose hobbies are most different to yours? How?
- Who has a similar job (or studies the same subjects) as you?
- Whose family is the most similar and the most different to yours? How?
- What unusual things have people in the group done?
- Who has done the most unusual thing?

May I introduce myself?

Introducing yourself via a first entry in a class blog

Tools ▼ Class blog
▼ Email

Technique

- Prepare an introductory entry for yourself in the class blog. Include any or all of the following:
  - A photo of you
  - A mini-biography of you
  - A paragraph about things you like and dislike

- Add this to the class blog and give it a title (eg *All about me*, or your name).

- Direct your learners to the page of the blog with your introduction on it, for example by email.
  - They read your entry.
  - They post one comment on it. This could be a question, or a simple response to something they have read about you.

- Respond to these comments in the blog as they come up.

- The learners can now write their own first entry in the same blog. They should give their entry a title and post it to the blog.

- Encourage them to read and then leave comments on each other's first entries.

Variation

The first entry in a class blog does not have to be a simple introduction. There are some other topics suggested in the box below.

Comment

You can make leaving comments on other learners' entries obligatory by including this in the task instructions – for example, 'Choose three of your classmates' entries and leave one comment on each'. However, we have found it is also effective to allow comments to develop naturally.

- My top five … (places, foods, things)
- Things I like most and least (about my town, my country, learning English …)
- Something many people don't know about me
- My favourite website, and why I like it
- An English phrase that I really like

Hello, this is me

Introducing yourself online via video

Tools	
▼	Webcam or digital camera (or sound recorder or voice board)
▼	Course site or class blog
▼	Survey tool or Quiz maker (optional)

Technique

- Prepare a short video of yourself (anywhere from one to three minutes long) with a webcam or digital camera. There are some suggestions below for the type of information you could include in your video.

- Upload the video to your course site or to a class blog, and ask your learners to watch it.
  - They each record their own video introduction of themselves.
  - They use your video as a model and include similar information.

- They upload their videos to the course site or to the class blog. Alternatively, they could send their videos to you by email, for you to upload.

- Ask the learners to watch each other's videos to find out more about their course colleagues.

Variation

If the learners do not have a webcam, or are uncomfortable videoing themselves, you could do the same activity using a sound recorder or a voice board.

Follow-up

Once all the videos (or audio files) are in the course site or blog, or on a voice board, you could create an online quiz or survey about the information the learners have shared.

Comment

We don't recommend that the videos last more than three minutes each. The longer the video, the larger the file size (and large files are more difficult to upload to a site). Longer videos also take more time to download, and this can be especially frustrating for learners on slower internet connections.

- Your name and where you're from
- Some of the things you hope for during this course (eg 'to get to know everyone well' or 'to have fun' – as well as course objectives, such as improving speaking skills or learning new vocabulary)
- Something interesting about you (this could be an interesting or amusing anecdote)

My window, my world

Sharing photos of views

Tools	
▼	Digital camera
▼	Course site or class blog

Technique

- Prepare a short description of what you can see from your window at work or at home. If possible, take a digital photo of the view.

- Post your description and digital photo to your course site or a class blog. The view from Nicky's office window is in the box below.

- Ask your learners to prepare a similar description of what *they* see from their own windows at work or at home.
  - They take a digital photo of the view if possible.
  - They add their own descriptions to the course site or class blog.

- Ask the learners to read and add questions or comments about the other learners' photos. Encourage them to respond to questions about their own photos.

Follow-up

Extend this activity by asking your learners which operating systems (eg Windows, Mac, Linux) and browsers (eg Explorer, Firefox, Safari, Chrome, Opera) they use. If they have had experience of several browsers, which one(s) do they prefer, and why? This can be very useful information for an online course.

Comment

A common complaint of distance or online courses is that learners feel isolated and far away from each other. This activity will often make them feel physically closer.

Thanks to Valentina Dodge for the idea for this activity.

My precious …

Sharing pictures of personal objects

Tools
▼ Digital camera
▼ Course site or class blog

Technique

▢ Take a digital photo of an object which has some sentimental value for you, and is unusual or unique in some way. There is a list of suggestions in the box below.

▢ Prepare a short text of about 100 words, explaining why this object is important or significant to you.

▢ Post the digital photo of your object, and the short text explaining its significance, to your course site or to a class blog.

- The learners prepare a similar description of a significant object, and take a digital photo if possible. Alternatively, they can search for a similar looking object on the internet and include an image of that.
- They add their own object and text to the course site or class blog.

▢ Ask the learners to read about, and comment or add questions about, the other learners' objects. Encourage them to respond to comments and questions about their own objects in the course site or blog.

Comment

Integrating the use of photos and images into an online course is a good idea. These photos can be chosen by you to make your course site itself look more attractive, and the learners can also be encouraged to contribute their own photos and images via activities like this one.

Personal photos not only help personalise tasks, but also make things more interesting to read for others.

- A piece of furniture which has been in your family for generations and has some history attached to it
- A memento from a special trip
- A toy or good luck charm
- A picture drawn by a child who is important to you
- A piece of jewellery
- A souvenir from a trip or holiday
- A birthday card or gift you've received

Slidesharing

Sharing photos about you and your interests

Tools
▼ Digital camera/photos
▼ Slideshow site
▼ Course site or email

Technique

▢ Choose four or five digital photos which show something about you. These photos can show aspects of your home, family, where you live, etc, or a trip you have made, a past holiday or a significant event for you, such as a wedding or birthday party.

▢ Upload your photos to create a slideshow in a slideshow site, and provide a short text caption for each photo.

▢ Share the link to the slideshow with your learners in your course site, or via email, and ask them to watch it.

▢ Invite them to each find four or five photos showing some aspect of their own lives (give them the options suggested above). If they don't have access to their own digital photos, they could choose images from the internet.

- The learners set up their own slideshows, with their chosen images.
- They add short text captions for each image.

▢ Ask them to share the links to their slideshows in your course site, or via email.

▢ Ask the learners to visit each other's online slideshows and to leave a comment on each – nearly all slideshow sites will allow comments.

Variation

You can use sequential images in a slideshow to teach and practise language points such as narrative tenses, sequencing, describing processes, giving instructions on how to do something, etc. First create your own slideshow as an example, then get your learners to create their own and to share the links.

Comment

Slideshow sites are usually intuitive and easy to use. However, if you think that your learners may have problems using the site, you could create a tutorial document, with screenshots describing the steps they need to take to set up their own slideshow.

Alternatively, search the internet for ready-made tutorials about how to use the tool. Somebody has probably already produced a tutorial, or there may be one in the site itself that you can point your learners to.

On the map

Adding yourself to an online map

Tools
▼ Guest map site
▼ Course site or email

Technique

- Set up a guest map online, and provide your learners with the link, via your course site or by email.
  - The learners add themselves to the online map.
  - They also add a short '*Hello*' message, including one fact about their country/region, etc.

- Most guest map sites will allow learners to mark their country on the map and to add a few lines of text. Some sites will also allow them to add a picture of their country's flag.

- Ask your learners to read the other entries on the online map. Use this information later as a basis for a quiz about the group (eg 'Who lives in Cyprus?').

Variation
If you have a group from the same country, the learners can each have their own online guest map, and add the places that they have visited. Alternatively, they can add themselves to a group map to show where they would most *like* to go.

Comment
It is one thing to know that there are people from several different countries participating on your online course. It's quite another to physically *see* this on a map. Participant maps are very motivating both for learners and course tutors, and they provide another effective visual stimulus for your course.

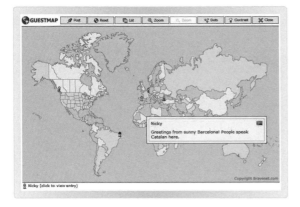

Sounds of me

Sharing favourite music with other learners

Tools
▼ Online music player
▼ Course site

Technique

- Prepare a short playlist of three to five songs you like, or which are especially significant to you. Add the songs to an online music player.

- In your course site, write the names of the songs you chose and the reasons you like them, or why they are significant to you. Provide a link to your playlist in the online music player.

- Tell your learners to read about the songs you chose. Ask them to listen to the songs in your playlist.

- The learners then create their own playlists of three to five songs each, in the same online music player. Include instructions on exactly how to do this if necessary.
  - They add the names of the songs they chose, as well as the reasons they like them or why they are significant, to the same place in the course site.
  - They also need to include a link to their individual playlists.

- Ask them to listen to each other's playlists and to read about their selections. They respond to, and comment on, each other's choices of music.

Variation
If using an online music player seems too complex, you can look for music videos of songs you like on a video sharing site (for example YouTube). Post a link to the videos in your course site and then ask the learners to do the same for their playlists.

Comment
Sharing personal music preferences tends to work well with learners of all age groups and levels. One danger in delivering content for learners online is that we can become very text-oriented. Including a range of media such as images, video and, in this case, music will enhance your online course content and provide welcome variety.

Sounds of you

Sharing sound effects via email

Tools
▼ Online music player
▼ Course site
▼ Email

Technique

▢ Choose a series of sound effects that you think are representative of you in some way. For some examples, see Box 1 opposite.
  • There are lots of sites with free sound effects you can download.
  • We recommend www.soundboard.com.

▢ Add the sounds to an online music player.

▢ In your course site, provide a link to your playlist of sounds. The learners listen to the sounds in your playlist.
  • They should try to guess what each sound is, and why you chose it or how it is representative of you.
  • They should add their speculations to the same place in the course site.

▢ Give the learners a link to the sound effects site you used. They then create their own playlists of sounds, in the same online music player. Include instructions on how exactly to do this if necessary.

▢ They provide a link to their individual sound playlists in the course site.

▢ Now assign each learner a partner. Give them the instructions in Box 2.

▢ When they have finished the pair work activity, ask each learner to write a short text (100–150 words) summarising what they heard, and what they have learned about their partner.

▢ The learners then post their texts to the course site. They must each read the summary about themselves and clarify why they chose the sounds, by replying to their partner's summary in the course site.

1

- Sound of Spanish guitar
- Sound of keyboard
- Start-up sound of computer
- Sound of wine bottle opening
- Sound of the sea
- Dog barking
- Children playing

2

- You will receive the name of another learner on the course from your teacher. This person is your partner for this activity.
- Go to your partner's playlist.
  ○ Listen to their playlist of sound effects.
  ○ Make notes of what you hear.
- Write an email to your partner.
  ○ Explain what you heard.
  ○ Guess why you think each sound is representative of them or important to them.
  ○ Ask *one* question in your email.
- When you receive an email about *your* playlist …
  ○ Read it.
  ○ Respond.
  ○ Answer the question that your partner asked you.

Follow-up
You can use the texts produced by the learners as a basis for further language work, or for a correction activity.

Comment
This activity provides a natural communication gap – the learners are keen to guess the sounds chosen by their partners and find out the reason they chose them. And it's a lot of fun!

What do you want?

Exploring course expectations in a group chat

Tools
▼ Course site or email
▼ Chatware

Technique

▢ Arrange a time to meet your learners for a real-time text or video-conferencing chat. Make the arrangements in your course site or via email.

▢ Ask the learners to note down two or three things they expect from you and from the course – before they come to the chat.

▢ Meet and greet them in the chatroom on the appointed day and time. Once everyone is present, start the chat with a few 'warmer' activities.

▢ Ask the learners, one by one, to paste their expectations into the text chat window.
  • Discuss each one with the group, either by text or audio/video.
  • Check if anyone else has the same expectations, and why.

▢ Make sure that all expectations are fully discussed and shared. Draw the chat to a close.

▢ After the chat, look through the text chat script where the learners posted their expectations.
  • Provide a summary of these expectations for the group.
  • State how you plan to fulfil them (if possible) during the course.

▢ Send the summary to your learners by email, or add it to your course site.

Comment

Real-time online chats are especially effective in giving the online part of your course a feeling of 'presence' and in helping a group to gel online.

The first time you hold an online chat, whether it is using text or audio/video chatware, it's best for all the group to be present if possible. If you think your learners may have difficulties with the chatware, you can prepare a print tutorial for them, with screenshots that illustrate how to access and use the chatroom.

Things in common

Finding similarities with a colleague in a pair work chat

Tools
▼ Course site or email
▼ Chatware

Technique

▢ Put your learners into pairs, and tell each pair that they must meet over the next week in real-time in the course chatroom. They will need to meet for about 20 minutes, and find as many things as possible that *they have in common*. There are some suggested topics you can give your learners in the box below. Inform them of all this in your course site or via email.
  • After meeting and chatting, the learners each write a short text (150–200 words) describing what they have in common with their partner.
  • They send the texts to you by email or add them to your course site.

▢ Provide a brief summary of one or two things each pair has in common, and share this with your learners in the course site or by email.

Follow-up

You can keep this information and use it to make a *'Find someone who …'* activity (see page 40) in the future. You can use the texts themselves to identify language areas for later study, or as material to create an error-correction activity for the group. You could also provide written feedback and correction on the individual texts for each learner.

Comment

To introduce your learners to real-time chats, it´s best to first hold one or two whole-group chats, such as that suggested in the previous activity. The next step is to set up pair work chats with a task like this one. Finally, you can set tasks for larger-group chats (see page 40 again for a group chat activity for four to six learners per group). This way, the learners will gradually be introduced to real-time chats and, by the time they do their first chat without the teacher present, they will be familiar with the chatroom and how it works. This will make it much easier for them to hold independent chats like the one suggested here.

• Age	• Studies
• Family members	• Favourite food
• Tastes in music	• Work
• Tastes in film	• Places travelled to

Find someone who ...

Finding others with similar interests in a small-group chat

Tools	
▼	**Course site**
▼	**Email**
▼	**Chatware**

Technique

◻ Your learners will be working in groups of four to six in an online chatroom. Assign them to groups and designate a group leader for each one. Inform the learners of these groups in your course site or via email.

◻ Each group of learners arranges to meet in your course chatroom at a time that is suitable to them all. The group leader will co-ordinate this by email and announce the final chat time to their group members by email.

◻ Prepare statements like the ones suggested in the box below. You can adjust these according to the level of the learners and their interests. Send the statements by email to all the learners a day or two before their chat.

- They have to find someone with each of the characteristics listed to complete a form. To do this, they will need to ask each other questions.
- They must try to do this in a period of 20 minutes, in the chatroom. The group leader is responsible for keeping the chat on track.

◻ Read the chat transcripts (for text chat) or listen to/watch the chat recording (for audio/video chat) of each group. Take notes while you watch, and summarise any interesting points that arise from the different groups (eg if everyone liked the same television show). You can also note down any general language points or corrections that are needed.

◻ Post your summary in your course site, or share it with your learners via email. Don't forget to congratulate the group on completing the task.

Variation

You can also ask your learners to write up their own summary of their group chat like this:

- *Mohamed has the same birthday as I do. We were born in March.*
- *Julia and Pamela live in the same city as I do. We live in Granada.*

The learners can then send you their summaries via email, or add them to your course site.

Follow-up

You can use the texts themselves to identify language areas for later study, or as material to create an error-correction activity for the group. You could also provide written feedback and correction on the individual texts for each learner.

Comment

As we saw in the previous chat activity, it´s best to introduce larger-group chats such as this one only after learners have experienced whole-group chats with you, the teacher, as well as independent pair work chats. This way, the learners will gradually be introduced to real-time chats and, by this stage, they will be familiar with the chatroom and how it works. This will make it much easier for them to hold larger-group chats like the one suggested here.

Find someone who ...

- lives in the same city as you do.   Name: _____
- likes the same television show as you do.   Name: _____
- had the same thing for breakfast as you did this morning.   Name: _____
- was born the same month as you were.   Name: _____
- wants to visit a country that you want to visit.   Name: _____
- has visited a country that you have visited.   Name: _____
- finds the same grammar point in English difficult.   Name: _____
- enjoys doing the same kind of classroom activities as you do.   Name: _____

Chapter 2
Reading and writing online

Activities

- Reading race
- Five clicks away
- Top tweets from history
- Short stories, short reviews
- Jigsaw tasks
- Follow that story!
- Blog log
- Class book blog
- Learner book blogs
- Blog diary
- Anti-protocols
- Your picture, my story
- Wiki city
- Wiki story
- One thing …
- I'd like some information …
- What happens next?
- Secret messages
- Podcast dictations
- Ready, steady, write!
- What about you?

Aim

These reading and writing activities aim to provide you with ideas that will encourage your learners to develop these skills by using a range of online tools. We refer you to a number of sites which can be used as prompts for both reading and writing, and to a number of Web 2.0 tools (such as blogs and wikis) which are especially effective for online writing.

Reading

This is one of the skills that is most highly suitable for online learning. Why? Firstly, the internet provides a wealth of reading materials, both authentic and especially created for language learners. Secondly, reading is an activity that is most often done individually, in silence (we are not considering reading aloud here). For these reasons, reading is often considered the 'easiest' skill to teach online.

Advantages
The main advantages in using reading material from the internet can be summed up as follows:

- A vast range of material is available to choose from.
- Content tends to be current and regularly updated.
- Texts from a variety of electronic media can be used – blogs, wikis, online dictionaries, visual media, etc – providing differentiation in terms of text type.
- Many learners, especially younger ones, will prefer to read online than from a book.

Interaction
Extensive reading is generally considered to improve learners' overall language skills, by exposing them to vocabulary and grammar. Texts on the internet are usually free, and there is plenty of choice for learners to read on their own, out of class time. However, apart from traditional reading activities based on internet texts, or extensive reading, there are ways to use online texts with learners in fun and interesting tasks, as a group:

- You can use online texts in real-time chat sessions, for example, and short online reading activities can be followed up by using a variety of other online media, such as blogs or wikis.
- You can use online reading activities to practise skimming and scanning skills. And reading a print book can lead to learners producing blog entries and then reading those of other group members.

Precaution
As with the reading of printed texts in a face-to-face context, the same issues of appropriacy of content, subject matter, type and level of text apply to online reading. In addition, with online reading resources, the teacher needs to ensure that recommended websites for reading materials stay current and up-to-date, and that links remain live.

Reading and writing online

Writing

The online medium also lends itself easily to the skill of writing. This can be done at the learners' own pace, in their own time (within deadlines!), and can be an individual, pair or even group activity when done online.

Advantages

The main advantages in getting your learners writing on the internet can be summed up as follows:

- They can do internet-based writing activities both in and out of class and at their own speed.
- There is a wide range of sites they can upload their writing to – blogs, wikis, posters, micro-blogs, etc.
- Their writing can be as short as a few words (micro-blogging or instant messaging in chats) or consist of longer texts (blog or wiki entries).
- Publishing learners' written work online can be very motivating for them – and it encourages them to write to the best of their ability.
- Some internet-based tools, such as wikis and blogs, lend themselves extremely well to collaborative or group writing activities.

Interaction

Writing activities do not have to be simply essays or texts written individually by learners in a word-processed document and sent to the teacher for correction. This is exactly the kind of traditional approach to writing that the internet-based writing tools we recommend can help us to get away from:

- Whether there is a place in your blended learning course for essay-style writing activity will depend on your course aims.
- The writing tools and activities we suggest are interactive and require input and/or responses from course colleagues.

Correction

An important issue for the teacher when dealing with online writing is that of correction and feedback. When writing a blog entry, for example, your learners will probably be concerned about accuracy; knowing that their work is available on the internet makes them especially keen to 'get it right'. You need to be prepared for this:

- You will be able to negotiate the level of correction that they need for their written work.

- You won't be able to rewrite their work entirely and correct every single error – but you *and* your learners should be clear on what levels of accuracy you both feel to be acceptable.

Feedback

Of course, feedback needs to be given not only on accuracy, but also on content – and this is where peer-commenting on online work can be invaluable.

- Learners can be asked to comment on each other's blog entries in the 'Comments' section.
- The issues of feedback and correction, and how to deal with these online, are also covered in the 'Liveware' section on page 27.

Reading and writing online

The internet provides a range of tools and content for practising both reading and writing. Rather than simply replacing paper with digital text, we suggest using the online medium to encourage collaboration between learners both in *consuming* text (reading) and in *creating* it (writing). What is more, online reading activities can often lead into online writing activities, and vice-versa.

We first look at activities that prioritise reading, and then at activities that prioritise writing. We start with activities that require learners to visit and read web pages.

- The first activities are web searching or web 'browsing' activities: the first is a fast search activity that takes place in real-time, the second encourages learners to browse at their own pace, and report back.
- The subsequent extensive reading activities use news sites and blogs.

Blogs lend themselves very well to reading and writing activities; we suggest activities that include reading and writing in blogs, and activities for writing in wikis.

Wikis can be an effective tool for collaborative online writing if used with appropriate task types.

- We suggest writing activities that use email, story and movie generator sites, and dictations.
- We suggest two short writing activities that can be used in real-time chats.

Reading race

Searching the web for solutions

Tools ▶ Chatware (text)

Technique

▢ Prepare 10–15 general knowledge questions (see the box opposite for some examples). Your learners will have to search the internet to find the answers to the questions as quickly as possible. Make sure *you* first research and note down the answers!

▢ Use a chatroom for this activity so that it takes place in real-time. Have your questions ready in an open word-processing document, so that you can copy and paste them into the text chat window during the activity.

▢ Meet and greet the learners in the chatroom. Explain the activity:
   - They are going to take part in a race to find the answers to questions by searching the internet.
   - You will put a question into the chat window.
   - They will use a search engine (such as Google) to find the answer as quickly as possible and type it into the chat window.

▢ Do one question first, to practise. Copy the first question from your open document and paste it into the chat window – copying ensures the pace of the activity is kept fast and the learners do not have to wait while you type out questions. Type *Go!* on the next line.

▢ The learners search the internet for the solution and type this into the chat window. Once everyone has typed in the answer, tell them if it is correct, and congratulate the group. Check that everyone now understands the activity.

▢ Copy and paste your questions into the chat window, one by one. Paste the next question only after the previous question has been answered, and you have given the correct answer (if necessary) and congratulated the learners.

▢ Give the learners five minutes to prepare two or three new general knowledge questions for the group (they need to make sure they know the answer too!).

▢ Repeat the procedure above:
   - They copy and paste (or type) their question into the chat window when asked to do so.
   - You then type *Go!* and the rest of the group searches for the answer.

▢ The learners each type the answer into the chat window. The learner who set the question tells them if it is correct.

▢ You nominate the next learner to type their question.

Variation

Prepare questions which illustrate a certain grammar point (past tense, indirect questions, common phrasal verbs, etc). Alternatively, prepare questions on a certain theme or topic (inventions, geography, art, history, technology) to introduce or recycle vocabulary or content.

Comment

The speedy nature of this activity makes it game-like which, in turn, makes it highly motivating. Finding accurate information quickly on the internet is also a very important skill in itself.

- Who was the 12th President of the USA?
- Who discovered penicillin, and when?
- Who invented the term 'blog', and when?
- What is the capital of [country]?
- How many players are there in an Australian Rules football team?
- Who designed St Paul's Cathedral in London?
- What is ANZAC Day?
- What is the temperature in Los Angeles at the moment?
- Can you translate the word 'run over' into your language.
- What is an 'Alsatian'?

Five clicks away

Going on a 'web browse'

Tools ▶ Course site

Technique

- Find a visually attractive web page on a topic of general interest to your learners. Choose one that has several links on the page, preferably in one area of the page (eg down the left-hand side, or tabs across the top). A news or magazine site will work well, or a site on a specific topic, such as the World Wildlife Fund, a film or book review site, or a city travel guide.

- In your course site, explain the activity to the learners:
  - They can take five clicks *away* from that page, following any link that looks interesting.
  - They can click only a total of five times!

  Give the learners the address of the web page and the instructions in the box below.

- The learners need to take a screenshot of the page where they end up after five clicks.
  - They post this screenshot to your course site.
  - They provide a one-line summary of the page.
  - They briefly describe what steps they took (their five clicks) to get there.
  - They say why they took each of these steps.

- In the course site, look at which pages the learners ended up on, and if any of them ended up on the same page(s) or followed similar steps to get there. Provide a brief summary of this in the course site.

Comment

This activity will also give you an idea of your learners' interests and provide interesting avenues for future lessons.

- Go to the following website and spend some time looking around: [insert the website you want the learners to start from].
- When you find a link you would like to follow, click on it. That is your first click. Look around the new page and make a record of the address.
- Repeat the step above until you have reached five clicks. This is your last page.
- Take a screenshot of this page and add it to the course site. Include a description of the page, and the steps you took to get there.

Top tweets from history

Real and fictional historical tweets

Tools ▶ Course site
(Note: You do not need a Twitter account to do this activity.)

Technique

- Find a site or sites which have 'tweets from history'.
  - One example is 'Historical Tweets': http://historicaltweets.com/
  - Another is Twhistory: http://www.twhistory.com/

- Explain to your learners what Twitter is if they don't know (see the Comment below).

- Say they are going to read some 'tweets' – messages of a maximum of 140 characters – from history.
  - They visit the site you have chosen and browse through the tweets.
  - They must choose the top three tweets they liked and make a copy of them.

- They then post their favourite tweets from history in the course site, but without identifying the historical event.

- Ask them to read the others' tweets and write what they think the historical event or context was.

Follow-up

Ask the learners to create their own historical tweets from different important moments – in the history of their country, for example.

Comment

The 140-character limit of Twitter makes for a useful creative restriction on how much you can say. Remember that it is useful to examine abbreviations and short forms that are used in modern digital communication.

To find a list of up-to-date abbreviations used on the internet, type 'English abbreviations on internet' into a search engine.

Short stories, short reviews

Reading and reviewing short stories

Tools ▶ Course site

Technique

- Choose a short story you think is appropriate in level and interest for your learners. See below for a list of short story sites available at the time of writing, or search for 'short story website'.
- Write a review of your short story in no more than 25 words, saying what it is about and why you like it.
- Post the story link and review to the course site.
  - The learners read the story you chose.
  - They comment on your review.
- The learners now choose their own short story and write their own review, using a maximum of 25 words.
- They post their reviews and short story links to the course site, and read and comment on each other's reviews.

Comment

This is a short, achievable task (not a lot of reading, not a lot of writing) which could be used as a warm-up to further online reading activities.

---

http://www.short-stories.co.uk/
A collection of short stories

http://www.eastoftheweb.com/short-stories/childrenindex.html
Quite easy – a children's site

http://www.americanliterature.com/ss/ssindx.html
Classic American short stories

http://www.storybytes.com/
Great short stories, from one word to 2048 words

http://davidbdale.wordpress.com/
Very short novels (299 words maximum)

Jigsaw tasks

Approaching news in different ways

Tools ▼ Course site
▼ Email

Technique

- Find an interesting short news story on the internet and note the link.
- Put your learners into three groups: A, B and C. Give them the link to the news story and ask them to read the article. When they finish, they will have a different task to do, depending on the group they are in. Post the instructions in the box below.
- Each group works together (eg via email) to agree and write one answer to their task.
- The learners do the task, post it to the course site and read each other's answers.
- Provide a summary of the activity in your course site, by giving feedback both on the content of the task answers and any recurrent language errors.

Comment

If the groups are small (three to five learners), then the learners can do the task together, communicating via email and posting their final result together. In this case, it's a good idea to assign a group leader to coordinate the work.

For larger groups, assign individual learners individual letters (A, B or C), and ask them to do the task individually.

Group A – Vocabulary work
Find four to six words that you think are important to the text and useful to know. For each word, find a definition and make your own logical and grammatically-correct sentence containing the word.

Group B – Story summary
Prepare a short (50-word) summary of the text in English.

Group C – Connected stories
Find three connected stories to this news story in other news websites in English. For each connected story, post the web address and a one-sentence description of the story.

Follow that story!

Tracking a news story as it develops

Tools ▼ Course site
        ▼ Email (optional)

Technique

▢ Find a series of news websites in English and identify four or five popular news stories of the moment.

▢ Explain that the learners are going to 'follow' a news story for a week, to see how it develops.
  - You give them the instructions in the box below.
  - They follow their stories for the week, consulting different news sites.

▢ At the end of the week, they summarise their findings in writing, and send them to you by email or add them to your course site.

Follow-up

Once all the learners have sent their stories and photos, you could collect them in a document entitled 'News of the Week'. Use this document as a basis for revision of common errors, a lexical set or as a springboard for a more detailed writing activity.

Comment

The objective of this activity is to promote extended reading over a short period of time:
  - By keeping to the same story, the learners are more likely to encounter similar lexical sets.
  - By becoming familiar with these, they should find comprehension of the texts improves over the week.

- Choose a news story from [the teacher's list] below or choose one of your own, and make a note of it.
- Every day, look through the news sites for a new 'item' in your story. Read the item and make a copy of the web address. Write a one-sentence summary of the new item.
- You must consult at least three different news websites.
- Finally, choose one photo from a news site to go with your story.
- At the end of the week, post your news story along with the following:
  - ○ the photo
  - ○ the list of items
  - ○ the web addresses
  - ○ the summaries

Blog log

Following a blog and reporting on it

Tools ▶ Course site

Technique

▢ Prepare a list of popular blogs on the internet that are regularly updated. There are thousands and thousands of blogs out there, but you could narrow it down by searching for 'Top 25 blogs' or 'Top blogs for language learners'.

▢ Decide how long you want the learners to follow the blog. This will depend in part on the length of your course, although we recommend a minimum of one week for an active blog (which updates every day or every two days).

▢ Make a 'Blog log' for the learners to complete (see the box below for an example).

▢ Tell them they are going to choose a blog and follow it over a period of time.

▢ Post your list of suggested blogs. The learners must select a blog from your list, or another blog of their own choosing. You could recommend they use a search engine like Google Blog Search to research an area of interest (http://blogsearch.google.com).
  - The learners each announce which blog they are going to follow and begin their blog log.
  - At the end of the set time, they post their blog log to your course site.

▢ Ask the learners to read all the blog logs and choose another blog to follow, if they wish.

Comment

Reading blog entries is quicker than other kinds of extensive reading. It makes for a very achievable, periodic reading goal.

Your name:

Blog name:

Blog address:

Blog topic (what is it about?):

Blog entries you've read (you can cut and paste the link):

Title	Link	My reaction
		Liked it?
		Didn't like it?
		Interesting?

Overall summary of the blog:

Would you recommend this blog to others?

Class book blog

Reading and blogging about a book

Tools
▼ Class blog
▼ Course site

Technique

▢ Choose a book that the group as a whole is to read. This could be a set text for examination purposes, or it could be a novel/graded reader for general reading practice.

▢ Set up a class blog for your chosen book. The blog will be used for as long as the group is reading the book – this could be several weeks, a term or semester, or longer.

▢ In your course site, explain to your learners that their reading of the book will be accompanied by a blog project, and that they will be adding to the blog themselves. Ask them to choose a title for the blog (for example 'Our book blog' or 'Book blog: [Title of book]'). Once they have chosen a title, assign it to the blog.

▢ Put the learners into pairs or groups.
   • They read the book description on the back cover.
   • They write a short paragraph of about 100 words, speculating about what might happen in the book, and what the outcome might be.

▢ Each pair or group adds their entry to the blog.

▢ For each chapter of the book, assign a different blog task for the learners to complete (individually, in pairs or in small groups). (See Box 1 opposite for different ideas for blog entries.)

1

- A 75–100 word summary of the chapter
- The most interesting/surprising/weird/amusing/ unlikely thing that happened in the chapter
- What will happen next
- A diary entry from one of the characters about what happened (different learners or pairs could take different characters)
- An alternative ending to the chapter
- An image on the internet, or a song, that reflects the overall theme/topic/feeling/mood of the chapter. Add to the blog, explaining your choice.

2

Complete these sentences:
- *One thing I liked about the book in general was …*
- *The best character was … because …*
- *The most interesting part for me was … because …*
- *The least interesting part for me was … because …*
- *I would/would not recommend this book because …*

Follow-up
When the learners have finished the book, set them a short summary task for their blog entry. (See Box 2 for some examples.)

Comment
It is important to vary the writing activities for each chapter, so that the learners don't get bored. You can set one activity for each chapter, or get different pairs or groups to do a different activity for the same chapter.

Learner book blogs

Recommending different books

Tools
▼ Learner blogs
▼ Course site
▼ Podcasting site (optional)

Technique

▢ Your learners will need access to books in English that they are going to read. This could be a class library of readers, the learners' own books, etc.

▢ Tell them they are to each read a *different* book in English. They will be accompanying their reading with a blog project, and they will be adding to the blog themselves.

▢ They each set up their own learner blog.
   - As a first posting to their blogs, they write a short description of 100 words on what their book is about, from the information on the back cover.
   - If possible, they add copyright-free images to their posting, from the internet.

▢ Set clear deadlines for the learners to read the chapters of the book.

▢ For each chapter, assign a different blog task for the learners to complete. See Box 1 on page 47 for different ideas for blog entries.

▢ When the learners have finished their book, ask them to visit the other blogs and to leave one comment on each, stating one thing that sounds interesting about that book.

Variation
The learners can produce a regular podcast, summarising each book chapter as they read it.

Follow-up
From the other book blogs, the learners decide which book to read next. They can also vote in your course site:
   - Which book sounds the most interesting?
   - Which writer would they most like to meet?
   - Which character is the most likeable or disagreeable?

Comment
You should provide regular feedback and encouragement on their blog entries in the 'Comments' section of the learner's blog. They will feel more inclined to post regularly if they know that others are reading their blog. This is why it is also so important to encourage them to read each other's work.

Blog diary

Keeping an online journal

Tools
▶ Learner blogs

Technique

▢ Help your learners to set up a learner blog in which to keep a diary over a period of time. Give them a clear time frame for this project – for example, they will need to write one blog entry a week or every two weeks, for a term or a semester.

▢ Ask the learners to write their blog posts regularly. Their first post could be an introduction, in which each learner describes the following:
   - Home
   - Family
   - Town
   - Job or studies

▢ Provide guidelines or suggested topics for subsequent blog posts, which can reinforce or develop topics covered elsewhere on the course, or the learners can write about topics of their own choice.

▢ We suggest that you, their teacher, also keep a blog diary, posting as regularly as the learners do, as this will be motivating.
   - They regularly visit each other's (and your) blogs and leave comments.
   - You regularly visit and leave comments on *their* blogs.

Variation
Instead of writing blog entries as themselves, the learners can pretend to be a famous or fictitious person and post blog entries as if they are this person. An 'imaginary person' blog project of this nature can last from a couple of weeks to a term, or longer.

Again, encourage the learners to visit each other's blogs and leave comments – in the character of their own fictitious or famous person.

Comment
Depending on the level of your learners, you may want them to send you drafts of their first few posts for feedback on accuracy, before they post. Alternatively, pairs could correct or provide feedback on each other's drafts, before these come to you.

Anti-protocols

How not to do things!

Tools
▼ Class blog or course site
▼ Email (optional)

Technique

- Explain that a 'protocol' is a set of instructions or guidelines on how to do something. In this activity, the learners are going to write an 'anti-protocol' – a set of instructions on how *not* to do something.

- Post the sample anti-protocol in Box 1 in the class blog or course site.

- Ask the learners to leave a comment about it, for example by writing the 'correct' way of doing something about it.

- Assign them their own 'anti-protocol' (see the list in Box 2). In a large group, they can do this in pairs via email.
  - They post their anti-protocols in the class blog or course site.
  - They comment on each other's posts.

Follow-up

Ask the learners to choose an anti-protocol (not their own) and post a 'real' protocol about it (what you should really do).

Comment

Make sure the learners understand this is meant to be funny, and that they understand the meaning of the *anti*-protocol. We have had learners who thought this was *real* advice!

1

What to do if you have computer problems
- First of all, panic.
- Think that you have lost everything.
- Do *not* ask for help.
- Do *not* turn the computer off and then on again.
- Shout at your computer and hit the keyboard.
- Throw your computer away and buy a new one.

2

- How to improve your English
- How to study for a test
- How to have fun on a Friday night in your town
- How to behave in a job interview
- How to be organised

Your picture, my story

Other people's photos

Tools
▼ Class blog or wiki
▼ Email
▼ Photo sharing website

Technique

- Choose a photograph from the internet of an interesting holiday place. Add it to a class blog or wiki. (See the Comment below.)

- Tell the learners they must each find a photo of a place they would like to visit and send you the photos by email. Give them a time limit for this (eg three or four days).

- Once all the photos are in, upload them so they are all on one page (for a wiki) or one post (for a class blog).

- Assign each learner a *different* photo to the one they sent you. Give them the task instructions in the box below.
  - They write about 'their' holiday photos in the 'Comments' box (if you are using a blog) or on the page (if you are using a wiki).
  - They then read and comment on each other's descriptions.

Comment

This activity is a good review of past tenses. To start the activity, you can write an entry yourself about a photo, which will serve as a model for the learners.

- Look at the photo you are given. Imagine you went on holiday to this place last month.
- Write a 100-word entry about the photo. Start with the following:
  I took this photo last month when I was on holiday in …
- Include information about:
  ○ where you were
  ○ who you were with
  ○ what you saw
  ○ what you liked
  ○ what you didn't like
- When you have finished, check your work for errors and post it on our [blog/wiki] next to the photo you were given.
- Read the other holiday stories.

Wiki city

Collaborating to create a tourist guide

Tools ▶ Wiki

Technique

▢ Set up one class wiki for the group.

▢ On the front page, type the title of the project, and add some images of famous cities (or of the city the learners all live in). Create a number of new pages linked from the front page, one for each small group you will create.

▢ Explain the project to the learners and put them into groups of two or three. Each group will develop an information page about their town or city:
  - If they all live in the *same* place, each group can focus on one aspect of the city: sights, food/restaurants, cultural traditions, history, nearby attractions.
  - If they come from *different* places, they can work alone and prepare an information page about their own town or city.

▢ The learners access the wiki, and work collaboratively on their own city page, adding images and text based on their topic or town.

▢ Visit the wiki pages as they develop, and provide the learners with feedback and suggestions.

▢ Once they are happy with the final versions of their city information page in the wiki, ask them to visit the other pages and leave comments on each page.

Variation

This activity essentially uses one class wiki to collect information on several aspects of one topic, with pairs or groups working on each aspect. Depending on the learners, you can choose a topic which will be of relevance to them, and use the same project structure:
  - Business English learners could research different types of marketing – one type for each wiki page.
  - Teacher trainees could investigate different teaching methodologies.

Comment

With this sort of project, it's a good idea to give the learners a clear timeline so that they know the following:
  - When the first draft of the page needs to be ready
  - When you will provide feedback on the first draft
  - When the second and/or final draft needs to be ready

Wiki projects that have a clear aim and deadline tend to work better than projects with no clear end in sight.

Wiki story

Collaborating to tell a tale

Tools ▽ Wiki
▽ Email (optional)

Technique

▢ Find a number of images which can be used to create the key elements of a story. These images could include:
  - A location
  - A building/house
  - Two or three people

▢ Set up a wiki for your learners. On the front page of the wiki, type the title of the project and add the images.
  - Add the names of the learners in random order – this is the order in which they will contribute to the story.
  - Add when they need to contribute to the story by – you could set this at one contribution per day by adding the dates of consecutive days to each learner's name.

▢ Set an approximate word-count for their contributions (eg 100 words each).

▢ The learners contribute, each in turn, to the wiki story, based on the images you have put on the wiki page.

▢ Once they have all contributed, ask them to read the finished story.

Follow-up

Use the (corrected) version of the story as material for future language practice activities or dictations.

Variation

For large classes, or to get the learners working in small groups, you could set up several different wiki pages for separate stories, with different images for each story. In this way, the learners work in groups on their stories. Each story could have images to set the mood for a different theme:
  - Horror
  - Romance
  - Comedy
  - Cowboy western

Comment

Wikis are excellent tools for reformulating learners' writing. You can read and reformulate each contribution on the wiki page itself, simply by deleting and rewriting as necessary and saving your changes. For each reformulation that you do, ask the learners to look at the wiki 'History' tab to compare their original version with yours. Each learner can then email you a short report on what they have learned about their writing by doing this comparison.

One thing ...

A 'round robin' email

Tools ▼ Email
          ▼ Course site

Technique

▢ Send your learners an email explaining the activity. Each learner needs to complete a phrase (or a number of phrases) which starts with 'One thing ...' (see ideas in the box below).
   - Include in the email a list of the group members in random order – this is the order in which they will need to forward the email to the next person.
   - Include your own name last on the list so that the email comes back to you:
   John —> Jane —> Paul —> Jill —> Teacher

▢ The activity proceeds as follows:
   - John completes the phrase (or phrases) starting with 'One thing ...' in an email and sends it to Jane.
   - Jane completes the phrase(s), leaving John's original phrase(s) in the email, and forwards it to Paul, and so on.

▢ The last learner in the list forwards the email, which now contains everybody's completed phrases, to you.

▢ Copy and paste the answers to the phrase(s) and add them to your course site.

▢ This list can now form the basis of a discussion in your course site, with the learners explaining their choices.

Comment

If you are working with learners who have different levels of English, then arrange the order of emails so that the stronger learners participate first. This way, the 'weaker' ones will have several examples to follow. An activity of this sort can work well at the beginning of a course, while the learners are still getting to know each other.

> - One thing I love about my city is ...
> - One thing I'd like to do in the next five years is ...
> - One thing I've learned in life is ...
> - One thing you should never do is ...
> - One thing I'd like to do during this course is ...

I'd like some information ...

Email roleplaying

Tools ▼ Email
          ▼ Course site

Technique

▢ Put the learners into pairs (A and B). Tell them they are going to do a roleplay together. Give them the instructions and useful language from the box below.
   - Learner A starts the roleplay by writing an email to Learner B.
   - Learner B replies to the email, but leaves the original email at the bottom of their reply.

▢ They continue writing to each other until they have finished their roleplay.

▢ Learner A forwards the final email to you. It should include the previous correspondence underneath it.

▢ Use the complete email 'conversations' to give the group feedback as necessary. Ask the learners to post their complete correspondence to the course site, so as to share their roleplays with their course colleagues.

▢ Ask them to then visit each other's roleplays and to leave a comment on each, stating one thing they particularly like in the roleplay or one new thing they have learned from it (such as a new language item).

Comment

This technique can be used with any roleplay situation. Coursebook roleplays can easily be adapted. If you have any *authentic* examples of such an email exchange yourself, then these can serve as an excellent model for the learners.

> You are going to work in pairs, A and B.
> - A: You want information about B's city. You are going on a visit there for three days. You want to know:
>   o things to see at this time of year
>   o good places to stay
>   o an interesting day trip to take near the city
> - B: You work at the tourist information office for your city. Answer A's questions.
>
> **Useful language**
> - *I'm writing to find out some information about ...*
> - *I'd like to know ...*
> - *Thank you for your enquiry about ...*
> - *We recommend ...* (verb + *ing*)

What happens next?

The plot's the thing

Tools
▼ **A plot generator or story generator site**
▼ **Course site**
▼ **Email**

Technique

▢ Browse one of the plot or story generators from the list in Box 1 and decide which one you think is most suitable for your group. Copy the link.

▢ Tell your learners they are going to write part of a story, but they are going to get some help from the internet first. Give them the link you have chosen and the starting instructions in Box 2.

▢ After everyone has posted their story beginnings to the course site, explain the following:
  - They must choose another learner's story and write the next 75 to 100 words.
  - They cannot write on a story that has already been added to or is their own.

▢ The learners then go back to finish their original story and send it to you by email.

▢ Go through the stories and highlight any persistent errors. Send the texts back to the learners by email for them to correct. They post their completed and corrected story to the course site.

Follow-up

At the end of the activity, put all the corrected stories in your course site and ask the learners to read and comment on the ones they like best.

Comment

When you are designing test items for future activities, using sentences from the stories can help make the language more memorable.

1

http://www.maddogproductions.com/plotomatic.htm

http://www.archetypewriting.com/muse/generators/plot.htm

http://www.randomplots.com/
(only does plots from science fiction television series)

http://www.school-for-champions.com/fiction/random_story.htm

http://www.plotshot.com/
(includes random photos from Flickr)

2

- A plot generator or story generator is a program that automatically creates story ideas.
- Go to [one of the plot generators] and click on the 'Create' button to get a story idea.
- Copy and paste the story idea you created at the top of a word document.
- Write *the beginning* of your story, writing at least 100 words. You do not finish the story.
- Put your story idea and story beginning in our course site for others to read – and continue.

Secret messages

Hiding a quote in a film the learners make

Tools
- ▼ Movie creator site
- ▼ Email
- ▼ Course site

Technique

- Prepare a list of film quotes that you think are interesting and suggestive. There is a sample list below to give you ideas. You should have one quote for each learner.

- Tell your learners that they are each going to create a movie. Give them instructions on how to use the movie creator site.

- Tell them they can have anything they like in their movie, but it must include the quote you will give them. They must send the link to their movie to you first, by email.

- You watch the films yourself and send the learners feedback on how to improve the language, if necessary.

- Share the links to all the movies in your course site.
  - The learners watch each other's movies.
  - They try and find the quote 'hidden' in the films.
  - They post their guesses to the course site.

- Summarise and provide feedback as necessary.

Follow-up

You can provide the learners with a list of all the quotes, to research where the original quotes came from.

Comment

Providing a quote for the learners to work with helps them to get started but does not restrict their creativity in any way. Finding and guessing the hidden quote gives them a clear task to complete while watching each other's films.

Here's looking at you, kid. (*Casablanca*)

After all, tomorrow is another day! (*Gone with the Wind*)

I'm going to make him an offer he can't refuse. (*The Godfather*)

Luke, I am your father. (*Star Wars*)

No, Mr Bond. I expect you to die! (*Goldfinger*)

Show me the money! (*Jerry Maguire*)

It's alive! It's alive! (*Frankenstein*)

I never drink wine. (*Dracula*)

I'm sorry, Dave. I can't do that. (*2001: A Space Odyssey*)

Podcast dictations

Listening to and writing a short text

Tools
- ▼ Voice board or podcasting site
- ▼ Course site or email

Technique

- Choose a short written text for your learners, on a topic that will be of interest to them and at a level they will be able to understand. You could choose the text from an authentic source, or write your own.

- Record yourself reading the text aloud slowly and clearly, on a voice board or in a podcasting site.

- Give the learners the web address of your voice board recording or podcast.
  - They listen to it in their own time.
  - They transcribe the text.

- As feedback, provide them with a written version of the text, either as a word-processed document in your course site or as an email, so that they can check their transcriptions.

- The learners then produce their own short recordings for dictations for the rest of the class, and add them to the same voice board or podcasting site.

Variation

For your dictation texts, you could use short written texts or paragraphs from previous units in the coursebook, as revision for the learners.

Instead of short texts, you could use individual words as your dictation, such as vocabulary items or irregular verbs from previous classes.

Comment

Providing the learners with regular podcasts as dictations, once a week or once every two weeks, is a very simple and effective way to help them develop their listening and grammar skills.

Ready, steady, write!

Completing sentences in an online chat

Tools ▼ Chatware (text or audio) with shared whiteboard

Technique

- Set a time for you and your learners to meet in a chatroom.
- Once you have all joined the chat and you have greeted the learners, tell them you are going to do a mini writing activity.
- Explain the procedure:
  - You are going to give them the beginning of a sentence.
  - They are going to finish it any way they wish.
- Write the following in the text chat window, or on the shared whiteboard:

  I think chatting online is …

- Allow everyone to type their answers and respond to the statement.
- Once you have finished with the first sentence, give the next sentence stem:

  After today's chat, I am going to …

- Continue with two or three other sentence stems. See the box below for some more examples.
- Use the language produced in the activity to focus on any common errors, either on the spot or in a subsequent class.

Comment

This is a good warm-up activity for a group chat, as it gets everyone focused as a group – in chats there is often a tendency for several things to happen at once and for it to get quite confusing!

- I have always wanted to visit …
- I really can't stand …
- My idea of a perfect day is …
- One thing I've always wondered is …
- The best way to learn new words is …
- The hardest thing for me in English is …
- My favourite English word is …

What about you?

Interviewing each other in a chat

Tools ▼ Chatware (text)
▼ Email

Technique

- Put your learners into pairs (A and B) and send them a copy of the 'internet' questions in Box 1.
- They arrange a time to 'meet' in the text chatroom. They need to set aside at least 30 minutes.
  - Learner A interviews Learner B, using the questions as prompts.
  - Learner B types 'What about you?' at the end of each response.
  - Learner A answers the same question.
- At the end of the time in the chatroom, one learner makes a copy of the text produced and emails it to you.
- Go through the text and highlight any errors, then send it back to the learners for them to correct.

Variation

This can be adapted, of course, to any set of questions. Box 2 has an easy set of 'favourites' questions.

Comment

When giving feedback, always include a comment about the content of the chat conversation, don't just focus on errors. Be sure to highlight any *good* uses of language as well.

1

- How much time do you spend online every day?
- What internet browser do you use? Have you always used this one?
- How many emails do you send a day? How many do you receive?
- Do you have your own web page?
- What is your homepage?
- What are one or two of your favourite websites?

2

- What is your favourite part of your country?
- What is your favourite time of day?
- What is your favourite meal?
- What is your favourite drink?
- What is your favourite free-time activity?

Chapter 3
Listening and speaking online

Activities

- My favourite podcast
- What's my line?
- Two-minute lecture
- Now listen carefully
- Tongue twisters
- Your message to the world
- Slideshow
- My favourite website
- So what's your excuse?
- The answering machine
- How to …
- Listen to this!
- Definitions
- Mystery guest
- Web tours
- Round the world
- Interpreters
- Panel discussion

Aim

These listening and speaking activities aim to provide you with ideas for practising both these skills with confidence. We first look at sites that provide accessible content for listening activities before moving on to tools that allow you and your learners to create listening activities for each other. We then look at speaking activities for both individual 'turns' and speaking in a group using different kinds of chatware (audio and video).

Listening

The internet contains a wealth of listening materials, in both audio and video format. Many face-to-face language teachers regularly use the internet as a resource for up-to-date listening, and take internet-based materials into the classroom or point their learners to specific audio and video resources to work on out of class time. Often the challenge is to know *what* audio and video material to choose.

Advantages

The main advantages in using audio and video material from the internet can be summed up as follows:

- The material is up-to-date and topical.
- You can find authentic material (not specifically produced for language learners) as well as ELT-related listening materials for all levels.
- You can suggest professionally-produced audio and video podcasts for your learners to subscribe to.
- The material is often accompanied by worksheets for use both in and outside the classroom.

Sites

What listening materials are available online? The answer is – pretty much everything! We can first separate audio and video listening materials into two categories:

- *Language learning* materials – those created for and aimed at learners
- *Authentic* materials – those aimed at the general public, not specifically at language learners

As teachers, we probably want to provide a variety of both for our learners, even at very low levels. If we look at audio and video materials especially created in sites for language learners (and a great many of the sites are free), we can divide these as follows:

- *Level* – materials for specific levels, such as online exam practice activities for Cambridge First Certificate, or for IELTS or TOEIC exams
- *Topic* – materials on certain areas, such as those for business English learners
- *Age* – materials for specific ages, such as young learners

Many listening sites created for language learners are very comprehensive:

- They include activities, lesson plans for teachers, and even transcripts.

Listening and speaking online

- Some have audio content lasting more than an hour (an interview or lecture), others have audio which lasts for less than a minute (Idiom/Word of the Day).

Podcasts

A term that is often used in conjunction with online listening materials, a podcast is an audio file which can be downloaded to your computer or MP3 player and which is produced in the form of regular episodes. In the activity on page 58, *My favourite podcast*, we point you to several English language learner podcasting sites. What makes them special is that you can subscribe. If you have a podcast capture program (such as iTunes, Juice or Dopplr) installed, you can have podcasts delivered straight to your computer. How does this work?

- You open the podcast capture program, it automatically goes along to the website you are subscribed to, checks for new episodes and, if there are any, downloads them for you.
- You can then transfer the podcast from your computer to your MP3 player, making them ideal for mobile learning, or 'learning on the go'. Learners can listen to English podcasts on their MP3 players on the bus, while out jogging or when walking to work!

Speaking

Providing learners with online speaking practice is arguably the most challenging part of an online or blended course. There are, of course, many 'listen and repeat' activities on the internet, but we would categorise this kind of discrete item approach as 'language work' (specifically: pronunciation practice). However, there are also a number of freely available tools that you can use to get your learners speaking to each other, to you and to others, in English, via the internet.

Advantages

The main advantages in using the internet for online speaking practice include the following:

- Learners can have access to the teacher and to each other, outside of class time, via simple audio/video tools such as Skype.
- You can easily bring in guests to a group audio or video chat session – even in another country!
- You can record individual, pair or group speaking activities and save them for later analysis.

- Learners can build up recordings of their speaking activities as part of a learning portfolio.

Tasks and tools

To practise the skill of *oral fluency* online, we have two options:

- Speaking activities done by the individual and recorded
- Speaking activities (pairs and groups) using online communication tools

Remember that for all speaking activities online, whether individual or group, learners need to have speakers and a microphone or headset. However, the tools required for *individual* speaking and for *group* speaking activities are different:

- Individual speaking activities are recorded for course colleagues and/or the teacher, for example by using voice boards or making podcasts. In other words, the learners will need to record themselves speaking.
- Speaking online in pairs and groups requires they use audio or video chatware. In other words, they will need to speak to each other in real-time via the internet. There are a number of online tools that can be used for group speaking activities, from simple text and audio tools to more complex platforms that allow users to interact via audio, video, text chat, shared whiteboard and shared web browsing features.

Individual speaking activities

When considering oral fluency, what do both teacher and learner need to keep in mind to carry out the activities we suggest? Don't underestimate how challenging it can be for learners to record themselves in a foreign language:

- Because a recording is permanent and will be sent to a teacher (and possibly shared with course colleagues) learners will naturally want to 'get it right'.
- They will be concerned about accuracy: about saying things correctly. They will probably want to write down exactly what they are going to say, and to read it while they record.

So be prepared for this to be a slow, gradual process and to support your learners in the move away from scripted speech into more natural improvised speech.

- The first few times that you ask your learners to record short audio texts, allow them to do very detailed preparation, including writing things down, rehearsing and even reading their texts aloud when they record. Texts which are read aloud sound very unnatural, but it's important that the learners gain confidence in recording themselves, and they will need the support of the written word to help them in the beginning, especially at lower levels.

- As they gain in confidence and fluency, start to suggest that they use notes, key words or short bullet points only, to help them when they are recording. This will help them sound a lot more natural and to learn to start improvising during recording.

Group speaking activities

Group speaking activities (which can be used in a blended course but also in courses which are 100% online) require two or more learners to meet together online and interact orally, usually in real-time. This means paying attention to logistical details such as exactly *when* they are going to meet. If they are spread out across several time zones, in different countries, it's a good idea to negotiate times for speaking activities that will suit the majority in the group. This can be done via a forum, an online poll, or by email.

- In blended courses, teachers often use the face-to-face classes for most of the speaking practice. Yet there is still a place for online group speaking activities, for example as an ice-breaker activity and for additional speaking practice out of class time.
- In 100% online courses, speaking practice will of necessity be done online. Ensure that your online speaking activities include a variety of pair, small-group and whole-group activities.

It is not necessary for the whole class to meet online at once, although this is certainly one option. Instead, pairs can use the chatware and record themselves. The recording can then be sent to the teacher for analysis and feedback. If the pairs are unable to record themselves speaking, they can always take notes about areas of difficulty, or questions that they have about language use or vocabulary, and send these to the teacher after the activity, along with a written summary of their chat.

- A third learner can attend a pair chat and act as observer, noting down any issues, queries or doubts, and then send these to the teacher for feedback.
- It is advisable, though, that such chats are recorded now and again, so that the teacher can also provide learners with feedback on pronunciation, fluency, etc.

The ideal size for an online real-time speaking activity with a group is about six to eight learners.

- More than eight or ten people start to get unwieldy and difficult to coordinate, with learners finding it difficult to take turns and interrupting.
- You can always run the group speaking activities twice (or even three times) with groups of four or five learners each time.

Listening and speaking online

There is a huge range of listening materials for language learners on the internet – more are being produced every day – and listening is, like reading, one of the skills we often find easiest to cater for online. Hence we have kept our section about online listening short. The activities that we do suggest can be adapted for different levels with slightly different content (which you can find without difficulty on the internet) and are in that sense *generative* – rather than *one-off* and suitable for one specific class.

Providing speaking opportunities for learners is more challenging, especially if we want to focus on spoken fluency, rather than accuracy ('listen and repeat'). However, we shall see that, with a little planning and imagination, rewarding and motivating speaking activities can also be carried out online.

We first look at listening activities, then at speaking activities for individuals and for groups:

- We start with two listening activities which use generic sites already available on the internet – podcasts and movie trailers – and then suggest activities which use audio material created by you, the teacher (and possibly by the learners themselves).
- The speaking activities start with less demanding individual recording tasks such as tongue twisters, short dictations and giving opinions, gradually increasing in complexity up to creating 'how to' videos.
- The group speaking activities are similarly arranged, from less demanding activities (dictations and word definitions) to more complex tasks like live interpreting or online panel discussions.

My favourite podcast

Exploring audio podcasts and reporting back

Tools ▶ Course site

Technique

▢ Post the instructions in Boxes 1 and 2 opposite to your course site.

▢ When your learners have completed the task (browse, choose, listen, comment, post) ask them to read each other's reviews, and to leave a comment on at least two of them.
  - They 'adopt' a podcast and subscribe to it for a month.
  - They listen to the regular podcast episodes which are produced by that site.

▢ They should listen to at least four episodes during the month.

▢ At the end of the time, ask the learners to report in the course site two or three interesting things they have learned from their podcasts.

▢ Summarise and provide feedback as appropriate.

Variation

Give your learners a list of podcasts related to one theme, such as 'Business' or 'The News'. For higher levels, provide links to 'authentic' podcasts such as those produced by radio stations or TV channels.

Comment

This activity points learners to *audio* podcasts. You can also provide links to video podcasts (also known as 'vodcasts').

Vodcasts are often produced by TV channels and are examples of authentic materials – they are not produced for language learners. However, you can also find vodcasts produced for EFL/ESL learners by doing a search for 'ESL or EFL video podcasts'.

Note All of the podcast sites listed were live at the time of writing. You can search for more sites, or alternatives, by using 'ESL podcasts' as your search term.

A podcast is an audio file on the internet that you can subscribe to, download and listen to on your computer or MP3 player.

Here are some popular English language learner podcasts for you to listen to:

BBC Grammar Challenge
http://www.bbc.co.uk/podcasts/series/gc

BBC 6 Minute English
http://www.bbc.co.uk/podcasts/series/how2/

Breaking News English
http://www.breakingnewsenglish.com

China232
http://www.china232.com/podcasts.php

ELT Podcast
http://www.eltpodcast.com

English Conversation
http://englishconversations.org

ESL Business News
http://www.eslbusinessnews.com

ESL Pod
http://www.eslpod.com

Podcasts in English
http://www.podcastsinenglish.com

Splendid Learning
http://www.splendid-learning.co.uk/podcast

- Listen to at least three podcasts.
- Choose *one*.
- Complete the description below.
- Post it to the course site.

Name of podcast:
- Link:
- Topic:
- Why I like it:
- How often a new podcast episode is produced:

What's my line?

Watching and listening to movie trailers

Tools   ▼ **Course site**
            ▼ **Email**

Technique

▢ Find a website with several movie trailers. Two of the most popular sites are:
  - *Yahoo Movies*
    http://movies.yahoo.com
  - *Apple Trailers*
    http://www.apple.com/trailers/

▢ Choose five or six trailers for upcoming films that you think your learners will like.

▢ Watch each trailer and write the following:
  - Two lines of dialogue that are in the trailer
  - An invented line of dialogue that isn't in the trailer

▢ See the box opposite for two examples.

▢ Put the name and the lines of dialogue in your course site.
  - The learners watch the trailers and decide which lines they heard and which one isn't in the trailer.
  - They *email* you the answers, they don't post them to the course site.

▢ Respond by thanking each student by email as their answers arrive.

▢ Provide a summary of the correct answers in the course site. Ask the learners to compare the original answers they sent to you by email and to listen again to any trailers they got wrong.

Follow-up

Ask the learners to write a short paragraph about which trailers they think looked most interesting, and why, or which films they would like to see or have seen already. They post their paragraphs to the course site, or send them to you by email. Provide corrections and feedback as necessary.

Variation

You could ask the learners to make their own similar activity, based on trailers of films they choose themselves.

Comment

Learners usually enjoy watching film clips, and the advantage of using movie trailers is that the clips are short and therefore easier to work with. Even then, the dialogue in films can be difficult to understand, especially at lower levels. So if you provide three lines of dialogue, the activity simply requires them to recognise the lines from the written word.

Getting learners to produce their own three lines for a trailer is, of course, far more demanding as they need to recognise lines from the *spoken* word. For very low-level learners, choose trailers with the clearest spoken English as your examples – and don't use the Variation suggested above!

Watch and listen to the trailers for the films below. Which line do you hear? Tick the correct one.

Transformers 2

Fate rarely calls upon us at a moment of our choosing.   ☐

The transformation is complete.   ☐

What you are about to see is top secret.   ☐

The Twilight Saga: Eclipse

She's still human.   ☐

I know the consequences of the choice you're making.   ☐

Choose me. He's a vampire.   ☐

Two-minute lecture

You record it, they listen to it

Tools
▼ Voice board or podcasting site
▼ Email
▼ Chatware (optional)

Technique

▢ Choose a lecture topic for your learners. Prepare a short two-minute lecture with five or six comprehension questions. You could use a coursebook text, a text on the topic already on the internet, or a text you have written yourself. (See the example in Box 1 opposite.)

▢ Record yourself giving the lecture and add your audio file to a voice board or podcasting site.

▢ Include your comprehension questions at the end of your audio file (see Box 2 for examples). Alternatively, put them in writing in your course site.

▢ Tell the learners to listen to the lecture and to send you the answers to the questions by email.

▢ Provide general feedback and corrections as necessary, on the voice board or in the podcasting site itself.

▢ Ask the learners to each choose a topic of interest, or one that has been covered on the course to date:
  • They prepare a two-minute lecture.
  • They include five or six comprehension questions.
  • They record themselves giving the lecture, along with their comprehension questions.
  • They add their audio files to the same voice board or podcasting site.

▢ Set up a name chain (eg María ← Iván ← Pol ← Oscar). Each learner listens to the lecture made by the learner *after* them in the chain (María listens to Iván's lecture, Iván listens to Pol, and so on). They respond to the relevant comprehension questions by email to that learner, who provides feedback on correct or incorrect answers.

Variation

Using video chatware, give your lecture as a *live* lecture with the learners 'present'. Record it for them to watch again at a later time, and as a model to prepare their own lectures.

For lower levels, ensure that your lecture is short, uses simple language and vocabulary, and is delivered slowly (but not too slowly!).

Comment

Listening to lectures is especially important for 'English for Academic Purposes' (EAP) learners, and you could use this activity with an EAP group several times during a course. You could also have your EAP learners listen to lectures on a variety of topics on the internet – the excellent 'Ted' series (http://www.ted.com) is a good resource for a non-specialist audience and includes native and non-native English lecturers.

The number 'three'

'3' is a special number. It is common in popular culture, science and religion. Some people say that in our minds we break concepts into three parts to understand them.

People say that luck, especially bad luck, comes in groups of three. There are famous threes everywhere. A hat trick is three goals scored by the same player in the same game. Athos, Porthos and Aramis are the heroes of *The Three Musketeers*, while Melchior, Balthazar and Gaspar are the three Magi (also called the Three Wise Men).

A trio is a group of three people or things that do things together, while triplets are three babies born at the same time from the same mother. Some people talk about the 'three Rs' in education: Reading, Writing and Arithmetic. We are supposed to eat breakfast, lunch and dinner, three meals a day.

Many books or films come in trilogies, which is a series of three. Finally, we live on the third planet from the Sun.

• What is a hat trick?
• What is an example of a 'three' from literature?
• What is the difference between a trio and triplets?
• What are the 'three Rs'?
• What is the last 'three' mentioned?
• Can you think of any other famous threes?

Now listen carefully

Following a series of instructions

| **Tools** | ▼ Voice board or podcasting site |
| | ▼ Email |

Technique

▢ Record yourself giving the instructions in Box 1 opposite in a careful clear tone, on a voice board or in a podcasting site.

▢ Direct your learners to the voice board or podcasting site. You could give them a gloss of words you think are difficult (eg *word-processing document, font, size* ...).

▢ Explain the activity to the learners:
  • You want them to listen to the instructions.
  • They must do exactly what they are told.

▢ The learners each email you their final document by a specified date.

▢ Respond by email, thanking each learner as you receive their document. When you have received them all, provide general feedback on how many learners followed the instruction to delete line 2. Point out that many mistakes on exams or official forms are made because the instructions have not been read carefully.

Variation

Adapt or create your own set of instructions for the learners to follow, with more or less complex instructions, depending on the level of the group.

Comment

This activity focuses not only on listening skills, and but also on the basic computer literacy skill of using a word-processing program.

You could include a 'Listen carefully' activity like this regularly on your course, for example every two weeks, in which you dictate instructions for creating a document, each time getting the learners to use different and progressively more complex word-processing functions. See Box 2 for a much more advanced activity.

1

1 Create a new word-processing document.

2 Type the following, each on a separate line. Use the font Times New Roman, size 14.
  Line 1: My name is
  Line 2: I have been learning English for
  Line 3: In my free time, I usually

3 Complete the sentences about yourself.

4 Now delete line 2.

5 At the bottom of the page, please type your name and the date. Use the font Times New Roman, but please type this in size 11.

6 Click on 'Save'. Give the document your name.

7 Email the document to your teacher.

2

• Create a new word-processing document.

• Open your internet browser. Go to Google Images. This is the address: http://www.google.com/imghp

• Type in the name of a city, eg New York.

• Choose one of the images that appear. Click on this. Then click on the text 'See full image'.

• The image should appear. If it doesn't, choose a different image.

• Right-click on the image and choose 'Copy image'.

• Go to your word-processing document and paste in the image.

• Now write two sentences about the image. Use the font Arial, size 14.

• Click on 'Save'. Give the document your name.

• Email the document to your teacher.

Tongue twisters

Recording tricky sentences

Tools	▼ Voice board or podcasting site
	▼ Course site

Technique

▢ Find a series of tongue twisters in English. There are many tongue twister sites on the internet, or you can use the suggestions in Box 1 opposite.

▢ Record yourself saying the tongue twisters:
- Read each one slowly and clearly once, then more quickly a second time.
- Add your recording, along with the text of the tongue twisters, to a voice board or podcasting site.

▢ Ask your learners to read and listen to the tongue twisters. They choose one and record themselves saying it *three times in a row*, each time trying to say it a little faster.

▢ They add their recordings of the tongue twisters to the voice board or podcasting site and listen to each other's.

▢ Begin a discussion on tongue twisters in your course site. Ask the learners to comment:
- Which tongue twisters do they think are the most difficult, the easiest, the funniest, etc?
- Why do they think tongue twister activities can be useful?

 1

She sells sea shells on the sea shore.

Toy boat. Toy boat. Toy boat.

Peter Piper picked a peck of pickled peppers.

Red lorry, yellow lorry, red lorry, yellow lorry.

Sam's shop stocks short spotted socks.

2

Specific sounds

/b/ and /v/
Vera Ball and Victor Black like veal and beer.

/w/ and /v/
Wanda is very very warm.

Initial /s/
The Spanish students are not scared of snakes.

Follow-up

The learners find their own English tongue twisters on the internet, and set one each as a challenge to their course colleagues in the course site. Each learner chooses a colleague's tongue twister, records it, and uploads the recording to the voice board or podcasting site. You draw the activity to a close by providing a summary of the tongue twisters chosen, and record yourself saying each of them three times, in one recording on the voice board or in the podcasting site.

Comment

Tongue twisters are a fun yet challenging way for learners to get to grips with the pronunciation of certain sounds and features of connected speech.

If you teach in a monolingual context, you could choose at least one or two tongue twisters which include sounds that you know are difficult for speakers of that language (see Box 2 for Spanish students). Always include one tongue twister that is not *too* difficult!

Because tongue twisters are written down for learners and they simply need to read them aloud, this is a good activity to start getting them used to recording themselves.

Your message to the world

Creating a short speech

Tools
▼ Voice board or podcasting site
▼ Video sharing site (optional)

Technique

Choose one of the 'Message to the world' topics from the box below and record your own answer to it. Adjust your answer to the level of your learners (for lower-level learners, keep your message short and use simple sentences and vocabulary).

Upload your recording to a voice board or podcasting site. If you are using a webcam, add your recording to a video sharing site.

- The learners listen to or watch your 'Message to the world'.
- They now prepare their own message, choosing from one of the options in the box below. They record it and upload it to the voice board, podcasting site or video sharing site.

Tell the learners to listen to or watch each other's messages. Set a task for when they listen to the messages, such as a worksheet with questions (*Who talks about world peace? Who talks about diseases?* etc).

Variation

Instead of preparing a worksheet with questions on the learners' messages, ask them to vote on which message is the most convincing/amusing/moving/realistic, etc.

Comment

It can be immensely challenging for learners to record themselves speaking in a foreign language. Make it clear that they don't need to speak for a long time.

For lower-level learners, just one sentence answering each of the questions in a message to the world is fine. For higher-level learners, you could ask for two or three sentences in reply to each question.

- What is your vision of a perfect world?
- If you could change one thing in the world, what would it be?
- What is the most annoying thing in the world?
- What is the best thing in the world?
- If you could say one thing to the world, what would it be?

Slideshow

Creating and narrating a slideshow

Tools
▼ Digital photos or images
▼ Slideshow site (with audio)
▼ Course site
▼ Email (optional)

Technique

Choose five images on a topic of interest to your learners.

Choose a slideshow site that records audio. Upload the images, and record yourself talking for about a minute or so about each image/slide. If the learners have low language proficiency, record yourself saying just one simple sentence or two about each image.

Add your slideshow link to your course site, or send it to your learners by email.

Ask the learners to watch your slideshow and listen to the audio. This will function as a model for them to produce their own slideshows.

- They should decide on a topic and find five images (on the internet, or using their own digital photos).
- They should use the same online slideshow site to produce their own slideshows, similar in length to your model.

The learners add the links of their slideshows to the course site with a brief description of the topic. For example:

This slideshow is about ...

They watch and listen to each other's slideshows and leave a comment on the course site for each, stating one thing they like about each slideshow.

Variation

A slideshow can allow business English learners to practise presentation skills. They prepare PowerPoint slides on a business-related topic, and record themselves as if doing a real presentation.

Comment

Creating an audio voice-over for a slideshow is an excellent way to practise presentations at a distance. You can then give personal feedback to each learner on their presentation, by email – or in a tutorial, either online or face-to-face.

My favourite website

Recording a tour of a favourite website

Tools   ▼ Sound recorder
▼ Course site

Technique

- Choose your own favourite website, and take a screenshot.
- Record yourself describing the website and your favourite sections of the site. Say why you especially like this site, and what you use it for.
- Add your screenshot and your audio description to your course site.
- Ask your learners to listen to your description and to leave a comment about it in the course site, stating if they think the site is interesting (or not), and why.
- They take a screenshot of their own favourite website.
  - The learners then record themselves describing their website
  - They say why you especially like it, and what they use it for.
- They each upload their screenshots and descriptions to the course site, with a brief one-line description of the website.
- The learners comment on each others' recordings, in the course site.

Variation

Choose two or three websites on a similar topic area, and take screenshots. In your oral description, describe just one of the websites. The learners listen to the description and identify which website is described.

Comment

You can ask the learners to use only sites in English, or in their first language. Encourage them to describe a website related to their hobbies and interests, rather than related to learning English.

By sharing their favourite websites, they are also sharing personal information about themselves, which will be interesting for their course colleagues.

So what's your excuse?

Different excuses for different scenarios

Tools   ▼ Voice board or podcasting site
▼ Course site or survey site (optional)

Technique

- Describe a brief scenario, in which your learners will need to each provide an excuse. See the box below for ideas. Outline the scenario in an audio message to a voice board or a podcasting site.
- Give the learners the link to the voice board or podcasting site, and ask them to read and listen to the scenario.
  - They think of the silliest or most outlandish excuses possible.
  - They record an excuse for the scenario.
- They listen to each other's excuses and leave a brief (written or spoken) comment on the voice board or in the podcasting site, about how original they think the excuse is.

Follow-up

Have a vote in your course site or via an online survey site, to decide which excuses are the most believable/unbelievable/original/outrageous/funny, etc.

Comment

Encouraging your learners to come up with outlandish or outrageous excuses for your scenario will provide a lot of fun as they think up original ideas, and this makes the activity a lot more motivating.

Thanks to Cristina Costa for this idea, based on her podcast in which learners give outrageous excuses for not having brought homework to class on April Fool's Day (April 1st).

- You have not brought your homework to class. What's your excuse?
- You arrived two hours late for an important meeting. What's your excuse?
- You borrowed a coat from a friend and lost it. What's your excuse?
- You broke a neighbour's window. What's your excuse?
- You forgot to meet a friend for lunch. What's your excuse?

The answering machine

Recording answerphone messages

Tools
▼ Voice board or podcasting site
▼ Course site

Technique

▢ Invent a character, including the following:
- Name
- Nationality
- Age
- Job
- Company

Add a photograph to go with the character.

▢ Record a message which your character might pre-record on an answering machine, and add it to a voice board or podcasting site (see an example message in Box 1).

▢ Introduce the character, for example by creating a fake profile in your course site or by describing the character in an email to your learners. (See Box 2.)

▢ Tell them that they each have 'an issue' with this character and their company (particularly in a business class, for example) – see some example issues in Box 3. Assign one different issue to each learner.

▢ Give them the link to the voice board or podcasting site, and ask them to listen to the answering machine message.
- They record their own voice messages, outlining their specific issue and stating a possible solution.
- They listen to each other's answering machine messages on the voice board or in the podcasting site, and the proposed solutions.

▢ Assign each learner a different issue or problem:
- They are now the character and must write an example email to the learner who complained, outlining what will be done.
- They share their example emails in the course site.

▢ Provide feedback on the learners' answering machine messages and emails, as necessary.

Variation

General English learners can leave answering machine messages for a friend, stating they cannot meet for dinner, or inviting the friend to a party, etc.

Comment

The activity as described above obviously works well in business English, as it includes not only leaving a message in a work context, but also writing a business-related email.

You could combine it with the more general task described in the Variation, and then work on register and formality by comparing what is more appropriate, in terms of vocabulary, structures and tone, for each kind of message.

1

Hello, this is Roger Andrews, Sales manager for Aussie Computers. I'm out right now, but please leave a message and I'll get back to you as soon as I can.

2

Name: Roger Andrews
Nationality: Australian
Age: 32
Job: Sales manager
Company: Aussie Computers

3

A delivery of stock has still not arrived.

The invoice for a delivery is for the wrong amount.

One of the staff was rude when he/she came to your office to collect a delivery.

An order has been lost.

How to …

Making 'How to' videos

Tools

▼ **Course site**

▼ **Email (optional)**

▼ **Video camera/webcam**

▼ **Video sharing site (optional)**

Technique

▢ Find five or six 'How to' videos on the internet. Try the following:
  - *YouTube*
    http://www.youtube.com
  - *Videojug*
    http://www.videojug.com

Use the ideas in Box 1 to help you search.

▢ Note down the video links, and share them with your learners in your course site or by email.

▢ Tell the learners to watch the different videos.

▢ In your course site, ask them:
  - Which video did they like best?
  - Which video did they find most useful?

▢ The learners now make their own 'How to' video on a subject of their choice.
  - They simply record themselves explaining to the camera how to do something.
  - Alternatively, they could film themselves giving instructions while doing it.

▢ Give them the ideas in Box 1 to help them.

▢ They upload their videos to the course site or to a video sharing site.

▢ They watch each other's 'How to' videos and leave one comment in the course site for each video, stating one thing they like about it.

1

Some sensible suggestions
- How to cook something/prepare a special dish
- How to use a specific computer program
- How to tie a tie/a particular knot/a shoelace
- How to fix something
- How to make a paper plane
- How to play a particular video game
- How to play a particular sport
- How to do a particular yoga position

2

Some silly suggestions
- How to ignore an acquaintance in the street
- How to cheat in an exam
- How to not pay for dinner
- How to pretend to be rich
- How to fall asleep in a crowded bus
- How to slip on a banana peel
- How to lose your homework

Comment

You can help the learners prepare for their 'How to' video by telling them to first divide the process into four or five steps. For each step, they need to prepare what they want to say, and what they will show in the video.

You can also brainstorm amusing or irreverent topics with them in advance. See Box 2.

You could even encourage them to create storyboards, and give them feedback on the language they will use for each step, before they record.

Listen to this!

Mutual dictations

Tools
▼ Email
▼ Chatware (text and audio)
▼ Course site

Technique

- Find a short text. This could be a joke, a news item or a short story (see the box opposite for an example).

- Keep the first sentence of the text for yourself. Send each learner a different sentence by email, keeping a note of who gets what.

- Set up a meeting time in your chatware. When the meeting starts, explain that the learners are going to do a dictation:
  - Each person will dictate a sentence in turn.
  - The others will all type it in the chat window at the same time.

- Begin with *your* sentence, and continue:
  - You nominate different learners to read their sentences. The other learners type each sentence in the text chat window.
  - You do *not* nominate learners in the correct order of the text.

- Correct each sentence as you go along, when necessary, either by pasting the correct sentence in the text chat window after the learners, or by verbally pointing out errors and soliciting corrections.

- When all the learners have read their sentences, tell them that these form a text. For homework, they must put the sentences in the correct order. Tell them that your sentence was the first one.

- Save the text chat transcript, or copy and paste the text into a word-processing document. Send this to the learners by email.

- The learners reconstitute the story and email it to you.

- Post the correct version in your course site, or email it to the learners.

Comment

This activity works well with the whole group. If you have a small class, you can assign two sentences to each learner. If you have a very large class, you can either look for a longer text, or divide the class into two groups, with one sentence per learner, but run the activity twice (once with one group, and again with the second group).

Even with a large group, because this is a dictation activity and all the learners are typing in the chat window, they are all engaged throughout.

> A man goes to his doctor because he hasn't been feeling well.
>
> The doctor examines him, leaves the room and comes back with three different bottles of pills.
>
> The doctor says, 'Take the green pill with a big glass of water when you get up.'
>
> 'Take the blue pill with a big glass of water after lunch.'
>
> 'Then, just before going to bed, take the red pill with another big glass of water.'
>
> The man says, 'Doctor, exactly what is my problem?'
>
> The doctor says, 'You're not drinking enough water.'

Definitions

Defining words for others to guess

Tools   ▼ Email
        ▼ Chatware (text and audio)

Technique

▢ Put together a list of words that your learners will know. These could be words from the coursebook, or words that have come up during the course so far.

▢ Send each learner one word by email.

▢ Set up a meeting time in your chatware. When the meeting starts, explain the activity:
  - Each learner has a word that they are going to have to define verbally.
  - The others must guess the word and type it in the text chat window.

▢ Do an example yourself to get started, saying your definition. When the learners think they know the word, they should type it into the chat window but *they mustn't say it out loud*.

▢ Give the learners a few more examples so they see how the activity works. Then review language for defining, by eliciting some of the structures you used to define your words (see the box opposite for some examples). Get the learners to type these in the chat window, or type them in yourself.

▢ Nominate a learner to define their word. The other learners listen and type their guess in the chat window. Make a note of any language problems in the definitions, for later correction.

▢ When all the learners have defined their words, recap by saying a few of the definitions yourself, and asking the learners to say the words verbally.

▢ For homework, put the list of words in your course site or send them to the learners by email:
  - They provide written definitions for each.
  - They send the definitions to you by email.

▢ Provide the learners with feedback on their language use from the chat session and the later homework definitions, with notes on common errors or particularly relevant points.

Comment

This activity works well with the whole group. You can make it as long or as short as you like, by limiting or expanding the number of words to define.

The activity can work especially well as a short warm-up activity for a group, and can be followed up by a more demanding online speaking activity for higher levels, such as *Interpreters* (page 71) or *Panel discussion* (page 72).

It's a noun/verb/adjective.

It's something you can use to …

It's good for + -*ing*.

You can usually find it in …

It means the same as …

A similar word is …

The opposite is …

Mystery guest

Interviewing a guest speaker

Tools
▼ Course site
▼ Email (optional)
▼ Chatware (audio)

Technique

▢ Tell your learners they will be interviewing a mystery guest. They will need to find out as much as they can about this guest in 30 minutes. See the box opposite for possible topics the learners can prepare questions for.

▢ Assign one of the topics to each learner in your course site or by email. They all need to prepare five questions before the interview.

▢ Set up a meeting time in your chatware. When the meeting starts, introduce your mystery guest (without giving much away!). The learners can briefly introduce themselves to the guest.

▢ Call on the learners by name:
  • They ask the mystery guest their questions.
  • The others listen to the guest's answers, and take notes.

At the end of the interview, thank both the guest and the learners.

Follow-up

After the interview, the learners do the following:
  • They prepare a profile of the mystery guest, using the information that they found out.
  • They also need to invent three extra things they think may be true of the guest.

They add their profiles to the course site.

Share the results with your mystery guest, and ask them to comment on the profiles in the course site:
  • How many of the invented facts were true?
  • How many were *close* to the truth?

The guest should also share a photo of themselves in their commentary.

Comment

This activity works well with the whole group. It's a good idea to only use *audio* in the chatroom, with no video being used. In this way, the learners only hear the mystery guest's voice, and they will be more imaginative when preparing the profiles. They will also be keen to see what the mystery guest looks like by the end of the activity.

• **Personal information**
Find out the mystery guest's name, age, family, where they live …

• **Work**
Find out where they work, what job they have, what they like and dislike about the job …

• **Free time**
Find out what they like to do in their free time, their favourite hobbies, what kinds of books or movies, etc, they like …

• **Unusual things**
Find out two or three things they have done in their life, and why they did them …

• **Food**
Find out what food they like and dislike, if they are a good cook, how often they eat out …

• **Animals**
Find out if they have any pets, if they like animals, if they have ever ridden a horse …

• **Travel**
Find out what countries or cities they have travelled to, when and why. Where did they go for their last holiday, where will they go for their next holiday? What is their favourite country or city, and why?

• **Further topics**
Their views on the environment, politics, education, sport …

Web tours

Taking others site-seeing

Tools
▼ Chatware (audio, video, shared web browsing)
▼ Email (optional)

Technique

- Choose a website you like, which will be of relevance and interest to your learners.

- Ask the learners to note down the link to their favourite website before the chat session. Tell them they will be giving their colleagues an online guided tour of the website during the chat, lasting three to five minutes.

- Set up a meeting time in your chatware. When the meeting starts, explain that you are going to show your learners *your* favourite website.

- Show the website:
  - Say what you like about each part.
  - Ensure that your tour lasts no more than three to five minutes.

- Ask one leaner to dictate the link to their favourite website, or to put the link into the text chat window.

- Show the learner's favourite website:
  - They tell you where to click, to show everyone around the website.
  - They explain what they like about each part of the website, for three to five minutes.

- At the end of the tour, ask the others to come up with one question each about the site. They can type their question in the chat window or use the audio to ask the learner their question. The learner answers their colleagues' questions verbally.

- Repeat the process with the other learners and their favourite websites. Make notes of any language problems, for later correction.

- Recap the names of the websites you have looked at with the learners.
  - They decide which website they liked the best (they can't choose their own!).
  - They type the name of the website they liked best in the chat window, when you say '*Go!*'

- Round up by pointing out which websites were the most popular, thank the learners and end the session.

- Send them feedback on their language use, with notes on common errors or particularly important points.

Variation

Instead of choosing a website, the learners can choose a favourite painting, cartoon, singer, architect, building, etc, and send an image of this to you, in advance of the chat session, by email. During the speaking session, upload each image in turn into your chatware, and ask the learner to speak about it, describing what it is and why it is a favourite.

Follow-up

The learners can write a brief description of one of their colleagues' websites, stating what they like about the site and what they are not so keen on. They send you their descriptions by email. Provide individual or group correction and feedback on the writing, as necessary.

Comment

This activity works well with the whole group. It's usually easier if you control the shared web browsing, and if the learner tells *you* where to click when showing everyone around. If they are confident with technology, you could assign 'moderator rights' to each learner in the chatware, and they could direct the web browsing.

If this type of shared web browsing is new to the learners, we suggest that you maintain control. You want to make sure that the technology goes as smoothly as possible, and to spend most of the online class time on the speaking activity itself rather than on possible technical aspects.

Round the world

Countries learners would like to visit

Tools	▼ Chatware (audio, shared whiteboard)
	▼ Email

Technique

▣ Find an image of a map of the world. Upload it to your chatware whiteboard.

▣ By email, tell your learners to note down the names of the five countries they would visit on a 'round the world' trip, starting from the country they are in now, and to bring these country names to the chat session.

▣ When the meeting starts, show the learners the image of the world map on the shared whiteboard. Using the screen pointer (if the chatware has one), show which five countries *you* would visit on a round the world trip, and explain why for each country. After each country, stop and ask the learners some questions about the country:
- What would *they* visit?
- What would they see?
- Where would they stay?
- What would they eat?

▣ Nominate a learner to describe *their* round the world trip. While they are speaking, indicate each country on the map with the pointer. Ask the learner to stop after each country, and ask the same questions to the rest of the group – What would *they* choose to visit, eat, see, etc?

▣ Repeat the process for each learner. While they are speaking, keep a list of which countries are mentioned and make notes of any language problems, for correction.

▣ Ask the learners which countries were the most popular, and which countries most learners wanted to visit. From your list, say the countries in order of popularity.

Follow-up

The learners imagine they really have visited these countries on a round the world trip. They post images and describe what they did/saw/ate/visited, and who they met, in each country. Send them feedback on their language use, with notes on common errors or important points.

Variation

Instead of a 'five country round the world' trip, the learners describe countries they have visited, countries they would like to visit, or countries whose food they especially like.

Comment

This activity works well with the whole group, and can be done with low-level groups for revision of structures such as *'I'd like to...'* or *'If I visited this country I would ...'*. The written follow-up provides irregular past simple practice.

Interpreters

Interpreting each other's speech in real-time

Tools	▶ Chatware (audio)

Technique

▣ Set up a meeting time in your chatware. Tell your learners they will be acting as interpreters at a meeting during the chat.

▣ When the meeting starts, put the learners into pairs (A and B) who speak the same language:
- Learner A is the speaker.
- Learner B is the interpreter.

▣ Give Learner A a simple topic and ask them to speak for a minute or two on it – in their *first* language:
- Learner A says every sentence in their first language.
- Learner B translates it into English, in the first person (*My name is Natasha*, rather than *She says her name is Natasha*).

▣ Give another pair the same task, but with Learner A speaking on a different topic. Ensure that the topics are simple, as translating live is challenging!

▣ Round up the session by thanking everyone and asking them to state one thing they found rewarding about the task and one thing they found difficult.

Variation

Ask the learners to do this task independently in pairs. Each pair decides on the best date and time to meet online. The pairs then report back on the experience in the course site, stating one thing they found rewarding about the task and one thing they found difficult.

Comment

This activity works best with a monolingual group, but can be done with multilingual groups if there are at least two learners who have the same first language. Translating live is extremely demanding, so it's best to avoid this activity with very low levels. Higher levels, however, can find it very motivating.

It's a good idea to get feedback from your learners about how they *felt* about doing the activity, afterwards.
- Did they think it was too hard?
- Would they like to do it again?
- Would they prefer to do it in a large group or in pairs?

Panel discussion

Talking together about a topic

Tools
- ▼ Email
- ▼ Chatware (text, audio, shared whiteboard)
- ▼ Course site (optional)

Technique

- Set up a meeting time in your chatware. Tell your learners they will be having a discussion on a particular topic. Send them the instructions in the box opposite by email.

- When the meeting starts, remind the learners how the activity will work. Nominate a learner to begin:
  - They give their opinion on the topic.
  - You help by asking a few clarification questions yourself about what the learner says and/or reformulation of language mistakes they make.

  Make a note of any main points they make.

- Nominate the next learner to give their opinion, and repeat the procedure.

- Continue this way until all the learners have given their initial opinions.

- Briefly round off this part of the discussion, copying and pasting onto the shared whiteboard the main points you noted down during each initial presentation. Give the learners a moment or two to reflect on these.

- Invite the learners to make further comments on the points raised. Encourage them by referring by name to points they have already made:
  - *Alberto mentioned how the internet makes us work faster.*
  - *What do you think of this, Olga? Do you agree?*

- Once the discussion has run its course, finish the activity and thank the learners for their participation.

Variation

When the first learner has finished giving their opinion, ask the others to come up with one question each for this learner. They can type their question in the chat window or ask the learner their question verbally. The learner answers their colleagues' questions verbally. Then the next learner gives their opinion on the topic, and the procedure is repeated.

Follow-up

Share a screenshot of the whiteboard summary of points you made with the learners, by posting it to the course site or sending it by email. Ask the learners to write a 'pros and cons' composition on the topic, and to send it to you by email. Provide corrections and feedback on their individual writing as necessary.

Comment

This activity work best with groups of four to six learners. If there are more than six learners in your group, we suggest repeating the activity with separate small groups. You can assign each group a different topic and record the discussion. The learners then visit other groups' recordings, listen to the different discussions and provide feedback to the whole group – on content, on points they agree with or thought were well made or they would like more information about.

We are going to hold a panel discussion on the following topic:

How is the internet changing the way we live?

- To prepare, make some notes about what you think.
- During the discussion, you are going to share your views.
- Be prepared to talk for at least one minute.

Our discussion will be on … [time and date].

Chapter 4
Language and evaluation online

Activities

- Name three …
- Binomials
- The lengthening sentence
- What's the next word?
- Online dictogloss
- Slideshow flashcards
- Spot the error
- Sounds in the clouds
- Grammar in the clouds
- Corpus work
- Create your mindmap
- Am I saying this correctly?
- Subtitle Oscars
- Resolutions
- Feedback questionnaire
- Class wish list
- Electronic portfolios
- Generating tests
- Yes we can!

Aim

This chapter begins with activities that provide you with ideas you can use and adapt to focus on areas of grammar and vocabulary with the whole group. They are followed by a selection of activities that both you and your learners can use to assess and evaluate progress on online courses.

Language work

As every language teacher knows, there is plenty of 'grammar' on the internet. In fact, many teachers automatically associate online learning with grammar exercises. However, as we have seen, there are many ways in which the receptive skills of listening and reading, and the productive skills of speaking and writing, can be taught online – and they can be taught through collaborative and engaging tasks.

The same is true of language work online. The nuts and bolts of the language – grammar, vocabulary, pronunciation – can be also taught through tasks that are both engaging and collaborative.

Self-study

Learners can practise phrasal verbs, tenses, prepositions, etc, via online quizzes which can include multiple-choice questions, gap fills, cloze tests, 'drag and drop' activities, matching activities and crosswords. But not only grammar can be practised in this way.

Vocabulary and pronunciation items are also well catered for on the web. Learners can match pictures with words, listen and repeat, classify words into groups by sight or sound, etc.

However, this 'discrete item' approach can also be found on most language CD-ROMs, and the approach is more one of self-study.

- Learners could in theory do these types of activities without even connecting to the internet, if they have the same material on CD-ROM.
- They could even print out and do many of the activities on paper.

Collaboration

There is of course a place for self-study and discrete item language work on any course, but in these pages we are concerned with language work that can be done online as *communicatively* and *meaningfully* as possible. The activities we suggest here are carried out *with the group* online, not by the individual. Although learners may in some activities be working with discrete language items, the focus is always on getting the group to work *together* on language. All of these language activities focus on encouraging learners to *use* language, and they take place in two ways:

- Synchronous (real-time) chat sessions, using either text and/or audio and video chatware
- Asynchronous (not real-time) tasks in your course site

Language and evaluation online

Advantages

Here are some advantages of doing language work online:

- Discrete item grammar, vocabulary and pronunciation activities allow learners to work on their own specific weak areas, in their own time.
- Group activities that prioritise collaboration provide learners with vital communicative practice.
- Online communicative language practice does not always need you to be present. Learners can record their synchronous interactions, analyse and review them, and send them to you for detailed feedback.
- By building up a bank of recorded language activities, learners can see their own progress over time.
- Activities offered in conjunction with a VLE allow for automatic or manual grading, and for a graded language profile of each learner to be built up.

Evaluation

Evaluation can be applied to many things: to course materials, to learners' work or performance, to the teacher. The words 'testing', 'feedback' and 'assessment' are also often used alongside 'evaluation', confusing the picture further. In this section we provide activities for all of these forms of evaluation and how they can be carried out online.

Tests

Teachers can make simple tests for learners by using online survey sites. Asking them to make online tests for each other ('learner-generated tests') can also be an effective way of revising course content. The learners can easily make their own tests with simple multiple-choice or true/false questions. Tests made with online survey sites will usually be discrete item tests – they will test single language points:

- They will be useful for revision purposes, as well as fun for the learners to make and then do.
- They will not be reliable indicators of learners' overall level of language proficiency.

Feedback

Feedback can be given online in variety of ways. We look at soliciting learner feedback via an online questionnaire (page 84) and via an online wish list (page 85).

- Feedback can be given *individually* by email, or *to a group* in the course site or in a blog posting.
- It can also be solicited from learners – on an activity, a course, even on you, the teacher.

Assessment

Learners can evaluate their own work and progress (self-evaluation), or present work to be assessed by others, such as their teacher or future employers.

- **Tests** can provide one source of evaluation for teachers, as we saw above.
- **ePortfolios** are a more holistic assessment of learners' work and are electronic portfolios. They are useful showcases of a learner's work over a period of time. You need to decide how you will use them:
  - *Formative* assessment – of ongoing progress
  - *Summative* assessment – of final achievements

Advantages

Here are some advantages of carrying out evaluation online:

- Discrete item tests can be automatically graded and the results entered into a learner's grade profile.
- Tests are easy to edit and reuse subsequently.
- Feedback can be stored and shared with others (school directors or parents).
- ePortfolios can showcase not just a learner's language achievements but also their electronic literacy skills (setting up a blog, creating audio and video).
- Electronic assessment data can be updated, edited, stored and shared with others. It can also be translated into other media (such as print) or imported into other platforms or formats (a VLE, an Excel spreadsheet, a customised school report).

Language and evaluation online

In this chapter, we suggest activities for online work which is collaborative, group-based, meaningful and engaging.

- We start with language activities that take place *synchronously* and focus on individual words, and then on language at the sentence and text level.
- We subsequently describe a number of language activities that take place *asynchronously*.

Next we look at activities which encourage learners and teachers to evaluate their work and progress on the course.

- **Goals** We start with *activities* to help learners set personal goals, and suggest several that can be used to solicit feedback half-way through a course. We also look at evaluation *tools* such as ePortfolios and tests.
- **Achievements** We end with an activity that helps learners identify their achievements and progress.

Name three ...

Reviewing and practising vocabulary

Tools
▼ Chatware
▼ Email
▼ Wiki (optional)

Technique

▢ Prepare a list of vocabulary areas your learners have been working with recently. Make sure there are as many areas as learners in the group – if there are eight learners, choose eight vocabulary areas.

▢ Meet and greet the learners and explain the activity:
- You will type an instruction in the chatroom starting with 'Name three ...'.
- They will all type in the answer as fast as they can.

▢ Do an example.
- You type 'Name three countries in Eastern Europe'.
- They type three countries as fast as they can.

If they are still not sure how the activity works, do another example.

▢ Continue the activity, choosing different vocabulary areas (there are some examples for lower-level learners opposite).

▢ Finally, ask the learners to scroll back through the chat text window, and ask different people to note down (on a piece of paper) the words that were given for different 'Name three ...' categories.
- Learner A notes down all the countries that the group supplied.
- Learner B notes down the shops.
- Learner C notes down the clothing.

▢ They send you their wordlists after the chat, by email.

▢ Collate the lists of words into categories and send the complete list back to the learners by email. Alternatively, ask them to add their wordlists to a wiki page.

Three shops
Three items of clothing worn in summer
Three items of clothing worn in winter
Three red vegetables
Three green vegetables
Three indoor jobs
Three outdoor jobs
Three pieces of furniture in the dining room
Three pieces of furniture in the kitchen
Three countries with two syllables
Three countries with three syllables
Three ways of greeting people

Comment

Fast-paced vocabulary review games like this can be a lot of fun. Although you will want to keep the pace of the activity flowing, make sure that you wait long enough between vocabulary areas to allow everybody in the group to contribute something.

You can insert comments while the learners are typing their responses, such as 'Nice one, Carlos!' or 'Interesting contribution, Sara!'. This is motivating for the learners, and also shows that you are reading and responding to their contributions.

Binomials

Chatting about collocations

Tools ▶ Chatware (text)

Technique

- Prepare a list of binomials your learners will probably be familiar with. Binomials are pairs of words that often go together – see Box 1.
- Meet and greet the learners in the chatroom and explain the activity:
  - You will type the first word of a binomial.
  - They will each type the other half of the pair as fast as they can.
- Do an example first.
  - Type *salt and ...* .
  - The learners should all type *pepper* (or another word they think goes with *salt*).

If they are still not sure how the activity works, do another example.

- Type in the first half of the next binomial (eg *black and ...*) and wait for all the learners to respond. They will not all come up with the same pair, and the results can be quite amusing.
- Recap the binomials which are most commonly used, and ask the learners to each type two binomials which were new to them in the text chat window.

Variation

You can use any word pairs for this activity – see Box 2.

Comment

Try to keep the pace of this activity fast; if you are not a very fast typist yourself, you can prepare your list of binomials beforehand in a word-processing document, and keep the document open during the chat so you can copy and paste your binomials into the chat window. You can prepare, and then copy and paste, the task instructions in the same way.

Using text chat is a very useful language activity. Because the learners are typing (rather than speaking), activities which focus on accuracy can work especially well.

1

salt and pepper	*bacon and eggs*
right and wrong	*left and right*
king and country	*king and queen*
black and white	*black and blue*
love and marriage	*love and hate*

2

- Infinitive and past tense irregular verbs (you type the infinitive of the verb, the learners type the irregular past simple form)
- Homophones (words which sound the same but are spelt differently)
- Synonyms and antonyms
- One-syllable words with the same vowel sound

The lengthening sentence

Working on grammar at sentence level

| Tools |

▼ Chatware (audio, shared whiteboard)

▼ Email

▼ Wiki (optional)

Technique

▢ Prepare a number of sentences that you want to work with. Arrange a chat with your learners in chatware that has a shared whiteboard facility.

▢ Meet and greet the learners. Type a short sentence on the whiteboard. For example:

John saw Jane in New York.

▢ Ask the learners one by one to add a single word to the whiteboard sentence to make it longer. See the box below for an example.

- How long can the learners make the sentence?
- As it gets more difficult to add a single word, allow them to add more than one.

▢ When the learners can add no more words, copy and paste the completed longer sentence into a word-processing document.

▢ Repeat the procedure with other sentences you have prepared. Three or four sentences are enough.

▢ While the activity is in progress, copy each completed long sentence when it is finished, to send to the learners later by email or to use in the suggested Follow-up.

Follow-up

Set up a wiki with one wiki page for each learner. Allocate one lengthened sentence from the chat to each learner. Tell them this is the first line of a short story. The learners write a story of about 150 words, using their allocated sentence as the first line. Give them a clear deadline to do this by.

The learners read each other's stories in the wiki, and add an observation in the 'Comments' section for each page, stating one thing they particularly like about the story. Provide feedback yourself, in the 'Comments' section too, for each of their stories.

Comments

You could focus your public feedback comment on each wiki story on content only. You could also provide individual detailed language feedback, by editing the wiki page yourself and directly correcting the text. The learners can then access the history of their page and compare their original story with the edits made by you, to see exactly what was corrected and reformulated.

A wiki's 'History' function is especially useful for peer or teacher correction of writing.

Learner A John *often* saw Jane in New York.

Learner B John often saw Jane in *downtown* New York.

Learner C John often saw Jane *rollerskating* in downtown New York.

Learner D John often saw Jane*'s brother* rollerskating in downtown New York.

Learner E John often saw Jane's brother *Chris* rollerskating in downtown New York.

Learner F John *very* often saw Jane's brother Chris rollerskating in downtown New York.

Learner G John very often saw Jane's *younger* brother Chris rollerskating in downtown New York.

Learner H John very often saw Jane's younger brother Chris *going* rollerskating in downtown New York.

What's the next word?

Chatting about chunks

Tools ▶ Chatware (text)

Technique

- Select a series of sentences or a short text you want your learners to work with. (See the box below for examples for a lower-level group.)
- Set a time for your learners to meet in the chatroom.
- Meet and greet the learners and explain the activity:
    - You are going to type the first part of a sentence.
    - They are going to type what they think the next word (or words) is.
- Type your sentence and stop. For example:
    Would you like me …
- The learners type what they think the next word is. Allow different learners to answer, before you say what is correct.
- Type the sentence again [*Would you like me to …*] including the missing word, and continue.
- In future sessions, ask the learners to each bring a sentence and repeat the same procedure, with a learner leading the chat.

Variation

For learners studying English for Academic Purposes, you could use fixed expressions that are typically used in academic lectures or academic writing.

Comment

It is best to stop and let the learners guess when there are a *limited* number of words that could go next. Formulaic language or fixed expressions work well: stop before articles, auxiliary verbs or participles, prepositions, or before common collocations.

Would you like tea or … [coffee]?

What time … [is it]?

Where do you come … [from]?

I'm sorry, I only speak a … [little English].

Have you got a … [pen]?

Please speak a little more … [slowly].

Could you repeat … [that, please]?

I don't know how to pronounce … [that]

Online dictogloss

Reconstructing a text together

Tools ▶ Chatware (audio, shared whiteboard)

Technique

- Arrange a chat with your learners, in chatware that has audio and a shared whiteboard facility.
- Prepare a short text (three to five sentences) to dictate.
- Meet and greet the learners and explain the activity:
    - They are going to hear you read a short text once, but only once.
    - At this point they must only *listen*.
- Nominate one of the learners as the 'scribe'.
    - The group will try to recreate the text from memory.
    - The scribe will write it on the whiteboard.
- Read the text once. Wait 30 seconds.
- As the learners begin recreating the text, do not help or correct them. After a few minutes, assign the role of scribe to someone else.
- If they are finding it difficult to remember and reconstruct the text, read it once more. Read it more quickly this (second) time.
- Let the learners work on the text together until they are happy with it.
- Post the original text on the whiteboard under the learners' text, and conduct feedback.

Comment

It is a good idea to create a text using structures and vocabulary that the learners will be familiar with. You could use a paragraph of a reading text from a previous lesson, or create a new text based on structures and vocabulary they need to review. It's important not to read the text too often – you don't want the learners to memorise the text word for word but to understand the overall meaning.

By getting the learners to try and recreate the text after only hearing it once, they will need to focus on accuracy. Allowing them time to try to recreate the text, before reading it a second time, means that when they do hear it again, they will be very focused on the vocabulary and structures.

Slideshow flashcards

Learning lexis and practising pronunciation

Tools ▶ Slideshow site (with audio)

Technique

▫ Choose an area of vocabulary you want your learners to acquire (eg clothes). Find pictures for each of the items in an online image site.

▫ Using a slideshow site with audio, load each image onto a separate slide. On the last slide, write all the new words as a list.

▫ For each slide, record yourself saying the name of the vocabulary item clearly twice.

▫ Direct the learners to the slideshow and ask them to watch it at least twice.
   - The first time, they should watch and repeat the words they hear. Tell them that all the words are written on the last slide.
   - The second time, they should do it without sound. For every image that comes up they must now try and say the word from memory.

They repeat this until they know all the words.

▫ Assign each learner a different vocabulary area you want them to learn. Give them the link to the image site you used. The learners make their own similar slideshows:
   - They use the same tool.
   - They put one image per slide.
   - They include the list of words on the last slide.

▫ If they are unsure of how to pronounce any of their words, they should check the pronunciation in an online dictionary. Check each presentation, and correct or clarify.

▫ The learners watch each other's slideshows at least twice, following the same procedure as above.

Comment

This kind of activity works well with lower levels, and with vocabulary areas that are easy to illustrate via images.

It is a good idea for all your learners to use *your* slideshow account. This way you can easily access and view the slideshows, and add the audio pronunciation of the new words to each slide. Lower-level learners appreciate having a clear model for pronunciation – the teacher. However, when they produce their own slideshows, by referring them to an always available online source of pronunciation such as an online dictionary, you are helping them to become a little more autonomous. They will learn that they can check pronunciation of items themselves online at any time.

Spot the error

Correcting grammar on a wiki page

Tools ▶ Wiki

Technique

▫ Prepare a short text of about 150–200 words which contains a number of typical language/grammatical errors your learners make. Choose the errors from samples of their writing. Make sure there are the same number of errors in the text as learners in the group – if there are ten learners, choose ten errors.

▫ Add the text to a wiki page. Ask the learners to visit the page and read the text to see if they can spot the errors (tell them exactly how many errors there are).

▫ Using the 'Edit' function of the wiki, each learner corrects *one* error only. Give them a deadline to do this by, and point out that the sooner they visit the wiki, the more errors they will have to choose from!

▫ Check that the learners have corrected the right item, and indicate any that they have missed or 'corrected' wrongly:
   - Highlight all the corrected errors in a different colour in the text, so that they are clearly visible.
   - Ask the learners to visit the page again and look at all the (now corrected) errors.

▫ They each prepare a similar 150/200-word text, including five errors similar to the language errors in the first wiki text.

▫ Set up a new wiki page for each learner. They visit their own new page and add their text with the five errors.

▫ Put the learners into pairs (A and B):
   - Learner A visits B's wiki page, and vice-versa, and corrects the five errors.
   - Learner A checks B's corrections, and vice-versa, and highlights in a different colour any errors wrongly corrected, or missed.
   - Learner B visits the wiki page again, and vice-versa, and corrects these outstanding errors.

Comment

You could summarise the activity by making a bullet-point list of the typical errors made by this group of learners, and adding the list to the front page of the wiki. The learners can refer to this list when doing future writing activities, or when revising for exams.

Sounds in the clouds

Studying specific sounds

Tools
▼ Email
▼ Word cloud site
▼ Course site

Technique

- By email, assign each of your learners a specific sound in English (eg /iː/):
  - They need to find at least twenty words with this sound.
  - They should try and include the sound in the middle, at the beginning and at the end of words, if possible.
- The learners send their wordlists to you by email. Check the lists to make sure the words all contain the right sound. Correct if necessary, and send back to the learners.
- Provide the link to a word cloud site and tell the learners to put their wordlist into a word cloud. Give them instructions on how to take a screenshot of their word cloud if necessary. (However, see the Comment below.)
- The learners post the screenshots of their word clouds, or links to the word cloud online, to the course site.
- Ask them to look at each other's clouds and decide what sound the words in each cloud have in common. They post their ideas to your course site.
- Check and provide feedback.

Follow-up

In a subsequent class, as a review activity, choose a selection of words from each of the word clouds, totalling about 30–40 words. Create a new cloud with these words. Ask your learners to look at the new word cloud, and to put the words into groups according to a common sound. They can post their groupings to the course site. Check that everyone agrees on the sound groupings, and correct and provide feedback as necessary.

Comment

Word clouds provide an appealingly visual way of presenting and reviewing vocabulary.

Word cloud sites usually allow you to store your word cloud online – in other words, you generate a link for your word cloud, which you can then share with others. This is an easier option than asking the learners to take a screenshot and to create an image of their word cloud.

Grammar in the clouds

Presenting a jumbled grammatical structure

Tools
▼ Word cloud site
▼ Course site
▼ Email (optional)

Technique

- Create a long sentence that includes a grammar point you would like to cover.
- Type it into a word cloud site and make a word cloud.
- Take a screenshot of the word cloud, or store it online and note down the link.
- Post your word cloud link or screenshot to your course site, or send it to your learners by email.
  - They have to make a sentence using all the words in the cloud.
  - They post their sentence to the course site or send it to you individually by email.
- In the course site, clarify the correct answer and highlight the grammatical structure you wanted to focus on.
- The learners then make their own word clouds for different long sentences that contain the target grammar. They post their world clouds to the course site, and try to make sentences from their colleagues' word clouds.
- Correct and provide feedback as necessary.

Comment

You can make your example sentence more or less complex depending on the level of your learners. With lower-level learners you could choose a structure including the negative auxiliary *doesn't*, simple adjectives or adverbs, and keep the sentence relatively short. With higher levels, you could choose a more complex linguistic structure, such as mixed or third conditionals, reported speech or question tags. You could even have two complex sentences in one cloud.

Proverbs in the clouds

- Proverbs and idioms can be quite challenging – and provide an interesting Variation.
- Choose some you would like to teach (not more than three or four), enter them into a word cloud site and make *one* word cloud.
- You can choose a common element – one particular word ('time') or one theme ('love'). You can give extra support by including definitions – but not in the word cloud!
- In a monolingual context, you can also provide equivalent expressions (if they exist) in the learners' language.

Corpus work

An online concordance for online research

Tools	▼ Concordance site
	▼ Course site
	▼ Survey site or email (optional)

Technique

 Choose a series of words that you would like your learners to work with. These could be:
- Verbs which follow a certain pattern
  (eg *manage, forget*)
- Adjectives that only go in certain positions
  (eg *awake, alive*)
- Common nouns that are used in many expressions
  (eg *hand, time*)

Explain what a corpus is (see Box 1). Assign each learner a word, and give them the instructions in Box 2.

The learners research their words in a concordance site.
- They post their findings to the course site.
- They include example sentences to illustrate their findings.

Respond and clarify any problems they have at this stage.

Summarise the main language points, based on the learners' findings.

Follow-up

Using the sample phrases the learners have found in the concordance, make correct and incorrect sentences. The learners have to choose which are correct. You could make this as a series of 'Correct/Incorrect' statements in a survey site, or simply send it as a word-processed document to the learners by email.

Comment

Your learners will probably be unfamiliar with concordances so it's important that you show them an example first. You will also need to show them where to enter their search term in the concordance.

You can select specific concordance lines and collate only those that you want. Show your learners how to do this as well: it will help them choose the most useful example sentences for their language point.

1

A corpus is a collection of language samples from people in real life. If you put a key word (such as *manage*) into a concordance site, it will give you a list of example sentences with the word. In this task, you are going to use a concordance site to find out about a word your teacher gives you.

```
e a color mixture as I can MANAGE. However, first I thoughtf
at as the writing poet can MANAGE, it is still great enough
dren. Do you think you can MANAGE it"? Mavis smiled. "I'll t
you. I don't know if I can MANAGE it tonight or tomorrow, bu
ve it, Phil. I think I can MANAGE one more favor for you". H
 "Oh no", she said. "I can MANAGE". She went ahead of him. O
not understand and cannot MANAGE, such as satire and irony,
February 1801, Oersted did MANAGE to experiment with physica
after much trouble he did MANAGE to get it back, he discove
them. Finally, Mercer did MANAGE to follow B'dikkat to the
stem. Many Hollywood films MANAGE somehow to be authentic, b
```

(from LexTutor: www.lextutor.ca)

2

Go to the concordance site and type in your word. You will see several examples of the word in a list. The lines in the list are called concordance lines.

Study the concordance lines and answer the following questions about your word:

- What kind of word is it? (verb, noun, adjective, etc)?
  Give examples.
- Can it be two different kinds of word (eg a noun and a verb)?
  Give examples.
- What words frequently come *after* your word?
  Give examples.
- What words frequently come *before* your word?
  Give examples.
- Are there any fixed expressions with the word?
  Give examples.

Post your answers and five example sentences for your word in the course site.

Create your mindmap

Grouping vocabulary items

Tools
▼ Mindmapping site
▼ Course site

Technique

▢ Choose an area of vocabulary you want your learners to learn or review, for example 'house' vocabulary. Make a list of 16–20 words that can be divided into groups within this lexical field (see some lower-level examples in the box below).

▢ Give the learners the list of words and explain the activity:
  • They have to make a mindmap of these words, organising them into groups they think are most useful or likely.
  • There is no one correct way of grouping the words.

▢ Give the learners the link to a mindmapping site.

▢ Each learner makes a mindmap, and saves it online or takes a screenshot. They post their mindmap links or their screenshots to the course site.

▢ Invite them to comment on and compare their mindmaps in the course site.

▢ Provide feedback and a summary of the different groupings which emerged in the mindmaps.

Comment

Learning new vocabulary is far more effective if learners are asked to work with, and think about, the words. Asking them to categorise new vocabulary into groups encourages this. It's especially important to tell learners that there is not one correct way of grouping the words.

By grouping the words according to their own criteria, they are creating their own networks of meaning, which will help them remember the vocabulary. They also enjoy comparing how others have grouped words and looking at the differences. The more learners work with, think about and revisit new vocabulary, the more likely they are to remember it.

house	bathroom	lamp	wardrobe
bedroom	kitchen	TV	bed
living room	dining room	sofa	armchair
coffee table	toilet	basin	fridge
shower	night table	cupboard	oven

Am I saying this correctly?

Spotting deliberate mistakes in a subtitled video

Tools
▼ Video sharing site
▼ Subtitle creator site
▼ Course site or email

Technique

▢ If you teach monolingual groups, find a short video clip or a trailer from a film in your learners' language in a video sharing site. A video clip of one to two minutes will be sufficient.

▢ Download the clip to your computer, or enter the video clip link into the subtitling site.

▢ Write English subtitles for the video clip. Include two or three deliberate mistakes, where the English translation does not match the *meaning* of what is being said in the native language.

▢ Send the learners the link to watch your subtitled clip:
  • They have to find the mistakes and write the corrected lines.
  • They then add the corrected lines to the course site, or send them to you by email.

▢ Change the subtitles in the film clip so they reflect the correct version. The learners watch the film clip again to see if they identified the mistakes correctly.

Variation

Instead of creating subtitles that deliberately contained mistakes in *meaning*, create subtitles that contain mistakes in grammar or vocabulary.

Comment

This activity is best for monolingual classes, and you will need to speak your learners' first language.

For lower-level learners, creating mistakes in your subtitles that focus on salient vocabulary will make the activity easier and more achievable. For higher levels, creating subtle mistakes in your subtitles that focus on slight differences in meaning will make it more challenging.

Subtitle Oscars

Subtitling a short film clip in English

Tools
▼ Video sharing site
▼ Subtitle creator site
▼ Course site or email

Technique

▢ Tell your learners to choose a short film clip of 2–3 minutes from a video sharing site that they would like to subtitle into English. The film can be in any language, even one they do not understand!

▢ Give the learners the link to a subtitle creator site:
  • They must each subtitle their film clip in English.
  • They add the link to their subtitled film clip to the course site, or send it to you by email.

▢ Check the subtitles, and make corrections or encourage the learners to self-correct as necessary.

▢ Once you are all happy with the subtitled clips, ask the learners to watch each other's. You can share the subtitled video links in your course site.

▢ The learners must nominate which video they think should get an 'Oscar' for best subtitles, and why. They can nominate any video but their own.

▢ The film clip with the most nominations gets the Oscar for 'Best Subtitled Clip'. You can award a 'virtual Oscar' by pasting an image of the Oscar statuette into your course post along with a summary of who won it and why.

Variation

You can award a number of Oscars in a number of categories to several film clips – most amusing film, most romantic film, most frightening film, most exotic film, etc. You could ensure that there are enough categories for everybody to win!

Comment

Some subtitle creator sites include film clips from obscure films and in a number of languages that users can subtitle for fun. This activity works well when the learners subtitle films from languages other than English.

If you work in a monolingual context, they could choose clips in their mother tongue and subtitle them in English – this is a *translation* activity.

If they choose film clips in a language they don't know and invent subtitles to match what they see on the screen, this is a *creative writing* activity.

If you ask them to subtitle film clips already in English, this is a *dictation* activity.

Resolutions

Setting and reviewing personal course goals

Tools
▶ Wiki

Technique

▢ At the beginning of a new term or semester, set up a wiki page and call it 'Resolutions'.

▢ Tell your learners that you going to make a resolutions list. Explain that a resolution is a personal goal or aim. On this list, they will make two resolutions each, to keep in mind for the rest of the term.

▢ Add some example resolutions to the wiki page (see the box below for suggestions).

▢ Tell the learners to access the wiki page:
  • They each add two or three resolutions, with their name in brackets after each resolution.
  • Under each resolution, they add how they think they can achieve the goal. Set a clear deadline.

▢ Check the resolutions list. Contact the learner directly if you need more information on a resolution.

▢ Provide a commentary on the list for the learners, on the same wiki page. Print out the list and keep it near your desk. During the term, check regularly with individual learners on how they feel their resolutions are going.

Follow-up

At the end of term, ask the learners to go back to the same resolutions wiki page and add another line under their resolutions, stating how far they feel they have achieved them.

Comment

Encouraging learners to set clear and achievable personal goals can greatly increase their motivation. It's helpful for learners if you set these goals early in a course and then revisit them periodically, to see how much progress has been made and what else can be done to ensure they are met by the end of the course. You can facilitate this process by providing advice on strategies that learners could use to achieve their goals.

This term I'm going to …

speak more in class. [name]

do extra grammar activities online in my spare time. [name]

write regularly in my blog. [name]

do some extra pronunciation activities. [name]

Feedback questionnaire

Soliciting mid-course feedback

Tools
▼ Survey site
▼ Course site or email

Technique

- Half-way through your course, decide what you would like to solicit learner feedback on (see the box opposite for some suggestions).

- Prepare 5–10 questions on the area you choose:
  - Make some of your questions closed (with a single answer).
  - Make some of your questions open-ended ('*Why?*' or '*What do you think of …?*').

- Copy and paste your questions into a survey site.

- Give your learners the link to the survey and ask them to complete it by a certain date. Collect and read the surveys.

- Take note of any areas that can be improved. Provide a summary of the survey findings for the learners, in the course site or by email, adding what you will do about any points that need attention.

Comment

It is always a good idea to solicit mid-course feedback from your learners, on both the face-to-face part of the course and the online part. Asking for feedback half-way through a course, rather than only at the end, gives you the chance to improve the course and deal with any issues or problems the learners may be having.

You can also create a questionnaire for end-of-course feedback, which will help you improve subsequent courses.

Content
- What areas of the course are you happy with?
- What areas would you like more work on?
- What areas do you think are being left out?

Coursebook
- What do you like/dislike about the coursebook?
- What activities do you like most/least?
- What other sources of material would you like to use?

Methodology
- What things do you like doing on the course?
- What activities do you like/dislike?
- What are you happy/unhappy about with the course delivery?
- How do you feel about the balance of online and face-to-face work?

Activities
- What did you like/dislike about activity 'x'?
- Would you like to do more of this type of activity?
- Why/why not?
- What other activities would you like to do?
- Do you have any suggestions for new/different activities?
- What activities would you prefer not to do?
- What activities work best for you face-to-face?
- What activities work best for you online?

Technology
- Are you having any technical problems with the online part of the course?
- Are you happy with the technical help you have received to date?
- What other help with working online would you like?

Class wish list

Providing feedback on class activities

Tools ▶ Wiki

Technique

- About half-way through your course, set up a wiki page called 'Class wish list'.
- Tell your learners that you are going to make a class wish list. In this list, they will tell you what they would like to do (and not do) during the rest of the course, both online and face-to-face.
- Add some example wishes (see the box below for suggestions) and tell the learners to access the wiki page.
  - They each add two or three things they would like to do (or not do), by completing the phrase *'I'd like to (not) …'*.
  - Give them a clear deadline for this.
- Check the wish list. You can see which learner has contributed which wish in the wiki's 'History' tab. Contact the learner directly if you need more information.
- Provide a commentary for the learners in the wish list on the same wiki page, acknowledging which wishes it will be possible to fulfill and which are not feasible, for whatever reason.
- As the course continues, plan activities which take into account the learners' wishes, as far as possible. Each time one of the learners' wishes is fulfilled, tick it off on the wiki page.

Comment

If you solicit feedback from a group, it's important that you then act on that feedback. Keeping a record on the wiki page of which wishes have been fulfilled is an effective way of showing that you are taking their suggestions and needs into account as far as possible.

I'd like to do more speaking activities in class, especially roleplays.

I'd like to do fewer grammar activities online.

I'd like to make another podcast.

I'd like to not have to write in our blogs every week.

Electronic portfolios

Creating electronic portfolios for evaluation

Tools ▽ Blog or wiki
▽ Email (optional)

Technique

- Decide what pieces of work your learners will be evaluated on over a term or year. (See the examples below.)
- Tell the learners that they will each create an electronic portfolio (an ePortfolio) in a blog or wiki, in which to store and present their work for evaluation. They will add work to their ePortfolio as the term progresses.
- Help them set up a blog or a wiki each.
- As the course progresses:
  - Indicate which pieces of work the learners should add to their ePortfolio.
  - Clearly explain the evaluation criteria and grading system (if there is one) for each piece of work.
- Evaluate each piece of work when it is added to the ePortfolio and provide detailed feedback to the learner (and a grade if necessary) by email, or in the ePortfolio itself in the 'Comments' section.
- At the end of the term or year, evaluate each learner's work overall, providing feedback on progress.

Comment

An ePortfolio is a useful showcase of a learner's work and progress over a period of time. There are different types of uses for portfolios – *formative* and *summative* – and you need to decide how you will use them. (See page 74.)

The aims and evaluation criteria for the ePortfolios must be made very clear from the outset. You could negotiate the evaluation criteria, as well as what pieces of work to include.

Completed portfolios form a useful record of learner achievements and, by having an electronic portfolio, work can easily be shared with parents (in the case of young learners) or future employers (for example in the case of university students or business English learners).

- Samples of written work
  (essays, book reviews, reports, letters, emails …)
- PowerPoint presentations
- Media created by the learners
  (audio/video recordings …)
- Online project work created by the learners
  (blogs, wikis, word clouds, online surveys …)

Generating tests

Creating online tests

Tools
▼ **Quiz maker**
▼ **Course site**
▼ **Email (optional)**

Teacher-generated tests

▨ Review the course content you have covered to date.

▨ Prepare 30–50 test questions for your learners. Questions can focus on language items (grammar or vocabulary) or on content from the course (history or geography, etc). See the box opposite for suggestions of question types.

▨ Put your test questions into a quiz maker that has automatic grading and give the learners the link to your test:

- Ask them to do the test and note down any parts that they have problems with or find difficult.
- Tell them to note down their test score and to keep it.

▨ Invite feedback on the test in your course site:

- Which items in the tests were the most difficult?
- Which areas do they feel they need revision on?
  - as a group
  - individually

▨ Provide feedback as necessary, and point the learners to extra online activities and resources in areas they identify that need more work.

Learner-generated tests

▨ The learners review the course content covered to date and prepare ten questions for their course colleagues.

▨ Give examples of the different question types that they can create.

▨ They can prepare their tests in pairs, deciding on their ten questions via email.

▨ Share all the test links in the course site.

▨ The learners complete a minimum of two or three of their colleagues' tests.

Follow-up
After a period of time (eg several months) you write another test for your learners covering the same or similar content, and using the same survey site. Ask them to do the test and compare their scores with the first test. In the course site, invite feedback on whether they think they have improved, and which content areas continue to be a challenge.

Comment
Quizzes are effective for creating discrete-item language-based tests. You will need to combine these types of tests with more holistic testing on the four skills, to ensure a comprehensive evaluation of your learners' overall language proficiency.

Fill in the gaps
Madrid ___ the capital of Spain.

True/False or Yes/No
This sentence is correct: *I do can swim.*

Multiple-choice
The people in Italy is/are friendly.

Matching
Match the infinitive with the past simple:

go	*bought*
have	*saw*
buy	*went*
see	*had*

Yes we can!

Reviewing course content and achievements

Tools
▼ Survey site
▼ Course site or email

Technique

- Towards the end of your course, review the course aims.
- Prepare a number of 'can do' statements for your learners (see the boxes opposite for some suggestions).
- Put the 'can do' statements into a survey site, creating a 'Yes/No' answer for each.
- Give the learners the link to the survey and ask them to complete the 'can do' statements about themselves by a certain date. Collect and read the surveys.
- Provide a summary of the survey findings for the learners:
  - Which areas do most learners feel they 'can do'?
  - Which areas do most learners feel less confident with?
- Provide additional resources for learners to review and work on the less confident areas.
- Post your summary to your course site, or send it to the learners by email.

Comment

The idea of 'can do' statements comes from the Council of Europe's Common European Framework of Reference: http://www.coe.int/t/dg4/linguistic/Source/Framework_EN.pdf

It reflects a functional view of language, in which learners learn to do certain things with language.

'Can do' statements reflect the ability to *use* the language, not just knowing *about* the language. They are also a good way of getting learners to evaluate themselves.

Lower levels	Yes	No
I can talk about myself and my family.		
I can describe my home.		
I can spell my name.		
I can ask for clarification.		

Presentation skills	Yes	No
I can give a presentation in English without reading it.		
I can make slides and use images and data to support my points.		
I can answer questions about my presentation from the audience.		
I can explain something in a different way if people did not understand me.		

Travelling	Yes	No
I can order food in a restaurant.		
I can ask for directions.		
I can ask for help and describe a problem.		
I can understand prices and communicate what I want in a shop.		

Using English social networks	Yes	No
I can complete a registration form.		
I can understand basic computer instructions.		
I can chat comfortably online in English.		
I can understand specific terms in online communication.		

Chapter 5
The finishing line

It is important to include an activity or two at the end of your online course to allow closure.

If you have paid attention to group dynamics and socialisation activities from the beginning of the course, the learners can feel a sense of loss at finishing and losing contact with course colleagues with whom they have worked closely over a period of time, even if exclusively online.

Activities like those in this brief chapter allow them to 'say goodbye' to the group in a supportive and fun way.

Before you go …

Your last class may be held face-to-face. Get the learners to do these activities just *before* the class – and then show and share the results by using a computer and projector in the classroom.

If you are finishing online in a blended course, you can also get the learners to do the activities online once they are home *after* the last class – and share the results online.

After you've gone …

Our final activity encourages learners to reflect on what they have learnt from the course and also suggests ways in which they can continue to work on their English once the course is over.

In this sense, you put the finishing touch to your classes but, at the same time, you point your learners towards a new phase in their language development – that of learning beyond the confines of the course.

The finishing line

You will see that our closing activities in Part B of *Teaching Online* cover a range of things which you and your learners can share and exchange online, moving from virtual gifts to messages and photos.

Whether online or f2f, it's important to finish a course on a positive note, and helping learners to articulate what they have learnt is one way to do this. At the same time, giving them directions for the future suggests that this doesn't necessarily have to be the end at all!

Parting gifts

A special something for the group

Tools
▼ Course site
▼ Email

Technique

▢ One or two weeks before the end of the course, set up an area in your course site called 'Parting gifts'.

▢ Send an email to your learners explaining the following:
- The course is coming to an end.
- Everyone is invited to offer the group a little virtual gift in the course site.

▢ If you like, send them the list of suggestions in the box below.

▢ Post the first gift yourself, explaining why you are giving it as a present to the group.

▢ Keep an eye on the discussion and post responses to the various gifts that are posted there. We do not recommend *forcing* others to post a response to this activity. It is supposed to be a nice, social 'finale' to the course.

▢ Once a few people have posted their gifts to the course site, send an email to the group highlighting what has been given. This should hopefully prompt the others to post something too.

▢ At the end, post a message warmly thanking the group for their gifts, as well as for all the hard work they have done on the course!

Acknowledgement We would like to thank Ana d'Almeida for the online version of this activity.

- A recipe for a favourite dish
- A photo of something relating to the course
- A video of them singing a farewell song or playing an instrument
- A poem
- A playlist of songs that they like
- A funny video from a video sharing site (eg YouTube)
- A link to an online video game
- A joke
- An online crossword or quiz
- A link to a useful website for future study after the course finishes
  (See *Take it from here ...* on page 90 for some ideas.)

Farewell message

A goodbye message to the group

Tools
▼ Voice board or podcasting site
▼ Course site
▼ Email
▼ Webcam and video sharing site (optional)

Technique

▢ Record a short 'goodbye' message to the group. Include some or all of the suggestions in the box below in your message.

▢ Add your audio file to a voice board or podcasting site, and put a link to it in the course site.

▢ Send an email to the learners:
- They should listen to your message.
- They should record their own goodbye messages on the voice board or podcasting site.

You could give them the suggestions in the box below.

▢ As they begin to leave their goodbye messages, send out emails to everyone telling them to listen to the messages. This should encourage those who have not yet left their message to do so.

▢ Once everyone has left a message, send an email to the group:
- They listen to all the messages again.
- You thank them one more time for their participation.

▢ Keep the voice board or podcasting site link, so that you can play it as an example for a future course.

Variation
Instead of using a voice board or podcasting site, use a video sharing site like YouTube. The learners record goodbye video messages with their webcams, and upload them to the video sharing site.

- Thank you to the group for all the work they've done
- Congratulations on coming successfully to the end of the course
- One or two things that you remember in particular about the course
- A suggestion for their future language development after the course finishes
  (See *Take it from here ...* on page 90 for some ideas.)

Photo gallery

An image to remember the course by

Tools
▼ Digital camera or image website
▼ Course site
▼ Email
▼ Slideshow site

Technique

▢ Find or take a photo of something or someone that you feel relates to the course in some way. See the box below for some suggestions.

▢ Add your photo to your course site and send your learners an email explaining the following:
  - What the photo is
  - How it relates to the course, for you

▢ Ask the learners to send you similar photos by email, each with an explanation of how it relates to the course for them.

▢ Once everyone has sent you a photo:
  - Put all the images together into a slide presentation using a slideshow site.
  - Add captions to each image, with the learner's name and some key words summarising how the image relates to the course for them.

▢ Send the learners the link to the slideshow site, thanking all of them for sharing their photos and thoughts at the end of the course.

▢ Create an area in your course site where the learners can comment on each other's choice of images and the key words.

- A photo of you in front of your computer
- A screenshot of all the learners' photos together (if they have shared photos)
- A beautiful image of something relating to the course you find online
- A collage of photos related to course content
- A diagram or drawing (made by you or found online)

Take it from here ...

Sharing what you take from the course

Tools
▼ Course site
▼ Email

Technique

▢ Write a short letter to the group in which you tell them what you have enjoyed on the course. Include some specific references to funny anecdotes, images or things that happened.

▢ Post your letter to your course site and call it 'What I'm taking away with me'.

▢ Send an email to your learners:
  - They should read your letter in the course site, and write a similar one themselves.
  - They should say what positive things *they* are taking away with them from the course.

▢ They write their letters and post them to the course site. They do not need to comment on each other's letters at this stage (although in our experience they often do, which is great!).

▢ Post a final comment, thanking everyone again for their contributions. It's worth also suggesting how they can continue learning beyond the end of the course, using online resources. There are some suggestions for keeping up their English in the box below.

- Listen regularly to podcasts in English. The BBC has a good selection:
  http://www.bbc.co.uk/podcasts
- Watch or listen to the news every day in English.
- Subscribe to and follow a blog.
- Find an English-speaking 'keypal' to write to, eg via *Language penpals*:
  http://www.languagepenpals.com
- Find a language exchange partner to practise speaking with online, eg via *Livemocha*, a free online language exchange site:
  http://www.livemocha.com
- Do another online or blended language course!

Teaching Online has suggested many ways in which internet resources, sites and tools can help you teach your learners online. But what about you, their teacher? Can the internet also help you to learn at a distance, without having to spend precious time and resources on professional learning activities such as travelling to conferences or attending teacher development courses? The answer is, yes it can. And in many ways, too. The advent of the internet has brought huge development possibilities to teachers across the globe.

Online development

Your development no longer rests in the hands of a few 'experts' delivering content – although there is still a place for this. With social networking tools, you can now have access to peers in other countries who are working in different contexts, and you can share tips and techniques, trials and tribulations with them online.

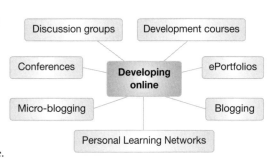

You can use tools that have been around for several decades now (such as email discussion groups) to keep in touch with colleagues, and you can use newer social networking tools (such as micro-blogging) to create and sustain your own personalised development.

Online opportunities

Exactly what possibilities does the internet offer you as a teacher? In Part C we suggest seven ways in which you can further your own professional development online – for free.

- Ways that use relatively older 'single' technologies
- Ways that use newer 'integrated' technologies

Our suggestions range from attending conferences online or setting up your own electronic teaching portfolio (or ePortfolio) to managing your own personal learning environment. For each of these, we outline what *forms* they take, we recommend what to do *first* to get started, we tell you how you can take things *further*, and we share a few of our own *favourites*.

Note You will notice that we look again at some communication tools you already encountered in Parts A and B amongst your *teaching* options, but now we examine how these tools can relate to your personal *development* network.

Discussion groups

The internet not only provides us with access to vast amounts of information, but also enables us to join online professional networks. There are a number of professional discussion groups for teachers online, which are free to join and which bring teachers interested in the same areas together from all around the world.

Forms ...

Discussion groups were one of the earliest forms of professional development available to teachers online, and many discussion groups still use simple email-based tools, such as Yahoo Groups. Increasingly, discussion groups are using more complex social networking platforms such as a wiki to complement the more traditional tools, but email-based discussion groups still remain popular and ubiquitous. This may simply be because an email-based group is an example of 'push' rather than 'pull' technology.

- *Push* technology delivers (or 'pushes') content to you – in this case you receive emails in your inbox from your discussion group.
- *Pull* technology requires you to go to an internet site to access information – for example you need to visit a group's wiki to contribute to it.

Push technology is in many ways more attractive than pull technology, because you don't need to do anything – the information comes to you. This is probably one of the contributing factors to the continued popularity of email-based discussion groups.

Online teacher discussion groups can vary greatly in their approach, content and aims. Although many groups claim to help teachers develop professionally, there are in fact very few that are fully-functioning 'communities of practice' – that is, groups that really *do* help teachers to develop by encouraging a reflective approach to their teaching practice, rather than simply providing teachers with lists of resources and information related to the profession. Online discussion groups differ in the way they function:

- They may simply distribute information – about upcoming conferences, scholarships, development opportunities and useful links and resources for teachers and other professionals.
- Some discussion groups will have sporadic periods of intense activity and debate, followed by months of silence.
- Others are active absolutely all the time, and can generate hundreds of posts a week, year after year.

Each of these types has its place and its utility. We personally find it useful to belong to a range of discussion group types – each brings something different to our own professional development. We recommend examples of the different types in the 'Favourites' section.

First ...

Join several (at least two or three) online discussion groups to start off with. Once you have been a member for a month or two, you will be able to see whether the group fits your needs and, if not, you can easily unsubscribe. If you join a very active discussion group that generates many emails every day, it's a good idea to set your subscription to receive a 'daily digest' of emails, to avoid receiving lots of individual emails from the group.

- The daily digest option means that you will receive one email per day, with all the group postings for that particular day in it. It makes managing a large flow of information from an active discussion group a lot easier!

Discussion groups

- If you belong to several groups, you will receive just one email from each group every day, which can also help you manage and sort through large amounts of information.

When you join a group, it may be considered good manners to post a short message:

- Introduce yourself.
- State briefly why you are joining the group.
- Explain what your particular interests are.

This is not true of all groups, so it's a good idea to first see whether other members have done this before doing so yourself. The two online 'community of practice' development groups we recommend in the 'Favourites' section will usually respond by welcoming you to the group if you post an introductory message.

For most teacher development groups, however, it is advisable to 'lurk' in the group for some time, in order to get a feel for the group and the norms of interaction and posting. 'Lurking' consists of reading posts, but not actively contributing. Once you feel comfortable, and have got a feel for the style and content of typical postings to the group, you could start to contribute yourself.

Further ...

Effective online teacher discussion groups, which we define as those that don't only *distribute* information but actually *contribute* towards professional development, will typically operate on a tacit 'give and take' principle.

- Group members are expected not only to take ideas, links, lesson plans, etc, from the group.
- Group members are also expected to contribute to discussions in which they have something of value to add and offer to the group.

Typically, also, these types of 'communities of practice' discussion groups will have a group of core members who post regularly, and then a large number of peripheral members who will contribute only sporadically, when they have something specific of value to contribute to the group. Whether you become a core member or remain a peripheral member of a discussion group is, of course, up to you.

If you are new to the group, and want to solicit advice on something or ask a question on a certain topic, it's a good idea to first look at the group archives, to see whether this topic has been discussed before. You may find that your question has been asked in the past, and the solution is already there in the archived posts.

Any online discussion group will expect you to observe the norms of 'netiquette' (or internet etiquette), such as showing consideration for others and respecting others' points of view. Below is a summary of what we consider to be the five most important netiquette 'rules'. You will see that they are not very different from the way we should behave offline in real life!

1 Always be polite and respectful of others.
2 Be supportive of online peers.
3 Acknowledge and respect others' points of view (even if you disagree).
4 Share your knowledge with others.
5 Be tolerant and forgiving of others' mistakes.

These netiquette rules mainly focus on interaction and behaviour. There are also a number of more technical considerations when contributing to an email-based discussion group.

- The first of these considerations is to avoid using capital letters when typing – this comes across as shouting, and is considered to be very bad manners!
- Another is to ensure that you use suitable grammar and spelling, and avoid using texting/SMS forms such as *i* (lower case) instead of *I* (upper case), or 'r u' instead of 'are you'.

Texting forms may be acceptable on some discussion groups but, in general, English teachers' discussion groups expect you to use standard English forms. You can consult the 'Liveware' section on page 27 for more courtesy rules.

Favourites ...

Two exemplary online teacher discussion groups which display all the characteristics of an effective 'community of practice' approach (both currently run in Yahoo Groups) are:

- **Webheads in Action**
  http://www.webheads.info
  A group of practising TESOL/TEFL teachers from around the world who discuss and try out ICT (Internet and Communication Technologies) in their own teaching, using the group to reflect and support their own development

- **Dogme**
  http://www.groups.yahoo.com/group/dogme
  A community of teachers who explore a 'minimal resources' approach to teaching and pedagogy, and apply this to their classroom practice

Discussion groups which run regular moderated discussions with invited 'experts' or guest writers are:

- **SEETA** (South Eastern Europe Teachers Associations)
  http://www.seeta.eu

- **British Council Teaching English**
  http://www.teachingenglish.org.uk/think/articles/guest-writers

- **IATEFL SIGs** (International Association Teachers of English As a Foreign Language Special Interest Groups)
  http://www.iatefl.org

Finally, the British Council lists below are discussion groups which disseminate information. They are helpful for keeping up-to-date on activities and developments in your own region. The scheme includes separate discussion lists for the following geographical areas: Africa and the Middle East; East Asia; Europe, Caucasus and Russia; India and Sri Lanka; Latin America; Central and South Asia.

- **ELTeCS** (English Language Teaching Contacts Scheme)
  http://www.teachingenglish.org.uk/eltecs

Development courses

An online teacher development course may take place fully online, or in blended mode (part face-to-face and part online). There are many online professional development courses, from short two-week courses on specific topics such as 'Wikis', 'Drama in the Classroom' or 'Teaching Young Learners' to full two-year (or longer) online and blended MA programmes.

Forms ...

Typically, an online teacher development course will be run in a VLE (Virtual Learning Environment) such as Moodle or Blackboard. Rather than relying on self-study, a good course should be group-based and tutor-supported, and lead to overt reflection on your classroom practice.

First ...

One of the most common problems that teachers face is how to tell whether an online teacher training or teacher development course is any good. Before you sign up for an online course, there are a number of questions that you should ask of the course providers – if the information is not readily available on their website. Below are the areas that we recommend you investigate. Of course, you may have other questions related to the course content, but these are questions that should help to give you an overview of the quality and scope of any online course, however short. But first:

- Check to what extent the organisation offering the training is reputable.
- Do this by investigating its website, by talking to colleagues and peers, or by asking other trusted sources such as established teachers' discussion lists for their recommendations.

Apart from these accreditation and validation issues, courses need to demonstrate current best practice in the field of online learning. In addition, for training or development to be effective it needs to be linked to *practice*, and involve some level of *reflection* on that practice.

- **Online delivery mode** How is the course offered online? Via a VLE, such as Moodle, or via an ad-hoc selection of tools, such as email and Skype? What provision is made for delivery of materials such as videos – are they online, or on CD-ROM? Is there a course start-date, and do you work in groups? What is the maximum and minimum number of participants on the course?

- **Course design** Does the delivery mode match the content? (If the course claims to help you improve and practise your pronunciation, but is delivered by email, it is unlikely to work!) How much of the course takes place *asynchronously* (not in real-time) and how much *synchronously* (in real-time)? Is provision made for both? How is the course content linked to your own practice, and how are you encouraged to reflect on this? How much interaction is there, and will it be with peers and/or tutors? What provision is made for getting to know course colleagues (online socialising) and for working in online groups/pairs?

- **Course materials** What materials are used in the course? Is a range of media used (text, audio, video ...)? Is a range of online tools used to deliver this content and to encourage reflection (online forums, wiki, blog, polls, quizzes and questionnaires, text and audio chat, video-conferencing ...)? Is a range of task types used – not just the old 'read and reflect' approach? Do tasks cater to a variety of learner styles? How?

Development courses

- **Tutors** Apart from having the necessary subject expertise, how experienced in e-learning are the course tutors? What demonstrable skills, training and experience do they have in this field? How much support can you expect from them, and what form will it take? How quickly will they answer queries and provide support? How much feedback and guidance on coursework or on progress is provided, and how? What is the tutor-to-participant ratio?

- **Requirements** What computer skills do you need to fully take part in the online course? For example, if you are expected to use Skype or video-conferencing tools, how much support will you be given to get up to speed with these technologies if they are new to you? Does your computer need to meet any minimum technical specifications?

- **Assessment** How will your coursework be evaluated and assessed? Will it include *formative* assessment (that is, ongoing) or *summative* assessment (for example, a final piece of work)? Will provision be made in the assessment mechanisms for online features of the course, for example your contributions to forum discussions?

- **Certification** Will you receive a certificate at the end of the course, and by whom will this be issued? Is the course offered or validated by a university or training body and, if so, is the certificate issued by them?

- **Feedback** And, importantly, what do others say about the course? What feedback from past participants is available?

A final word of advice: online learning does not suit everybody. Before you sign up to a long-term online course such as a two-year online MA programme, try a shorter online teacher development course of a few weeks or months, and see how you like it.

Further ...

As with any face-to-face teacher development course, how much you get out of an online teacher development course will depend to some extent on what you put into it. Once you have decided on a course to take and have signed up, you will need to manage your time effectively. In our experience, participants often find it useful to block out a few hours of time on a regular basis (eg a couple of times a week, depending on the scope and length of the course) to dedicate to their coursework.

One of the great advantages of an online teacher development course is that you are likely to work with colleagues who are in different parts of the world. So ensure that you take full advantage of the interaction possibilities provided by your course:

- Asynchronous forum discussions
- Blog and wiki contributions
- Synchronous video-conferencing sessions

This will enable you to not only engage more fully with the course materials, but to learn from your colleagues and build a deeper, more rewarding relationship with them and your tutors.

Development courses

Favourites ...

The kind of online course you decide to take will depend very much on your needs:

- Are you looking for an official qualification, such as a Certificate, Diploma or MA?
- Are you looking for a course on a specific topic, such as 'Blogs' or 'Motivating Learners'?

The vast majority of online teacher development courses which are tutor-supported are not free, for obvious reasons. Rather than recommend specific courses, we suggest that you do a Google search on a topic you're interested in learning about (eg 'blogs + online course'), and then investigate some of the links, using the questions in the 'First' section above to help you evaluate a course.

Electronic Village Online

However, one series of excellent free online courses, which are staffed by volunteer moderators, are the annual Electronic Village Online (EVO) mini-courses offered by the CALL Interest Section of TESOL USA.

TESOL USA offers the fully online EVO courses as a virtual extension of its annual face-to-face conference held in the USA. Anyone can offer to lead an EVO course, and anyone can sign up for a course.

The excellent Webheads group (see page 94) are usually very active in these courses, both as facilitators and as participants. EVO courses typically last six weeks, and past course topics have included:

Blogs
ePortfolios
Conflict Resolution for English Language Learners
Digital Storytelling
Teaching English with Drama
Tips and Tricks for Online Teachers
Virtual Worlds for Language Learning

You'll find a comprehensive list of past EVO course topics dating from 2001 here: http://evosessions.pbworks.com/EVO+Previous+Sessions

To check the courses currently on offer, simply google 'Electronic Village Online + [year]'.

Conferences

Attending a face-to-face conference requires time and resources. If the conference is being held in another country, it can require a significant amount of time *and* resources, and is often beyond the means of most language teachers. The advent of the internet has witnessed an increasing number of conferences offered purely online, many of them for free. Participants no longer need to spend time and money paying registration fees, taking time off work to attend or travelling long distances. With an internet connection, you can attend an online conference from your home or office.

Forms ...

How does an online conference work? What does it look like? Like a face-to-face conference, an online conference is a *synchronous* event, that is, it takes place in real-time and will have a programme with speakers. A short online conference may last a few hours or half a day, or it can last several days. Typically, the conference will be offered via a synchronous online platform, so that participants can hear and see the speakers, as well as their PowerPoint slides. Depending on the platform used:

- A speaker may be able to show web pages to participants.
- There may also be a collaborative whiteboard which participants can contribute to.
- There is usually also a chat window for synchronous text chat, where participants can interact with the speaker and with one another.

Apart from the presenter, there is often a moderator present, who introduces the speakers and may coordinate a Q & A (question and answer) session at the end of the online presentations.

First ...

The best way to find out about upcoming online conferences is to belong to a teacher discussion group, such as those recommended earlier. Online conferences are frequently announced online. They are also sometimes announced in teachers' association print newsletters, or you can sign up to receive online newsletters and updates from publishers who may offer regular 'webinars' (see the example of a webinar described in the 'Favourites' section). But by far the best way of keeping up-to-date with what's on offer for teachers online is to belong to any of the online teachers' networks we describe in Part C!

- You will need a broadband internet connection in order to be able to *see* the speaker on video. Video takes up a lot of bandwidth, and if you are on a 'dial up' connection, you may be unable to hear and see the speaker well. Some synchronous conference platforms will allow for an 'audio only' option, which can help those participants on limited bandwidth.
- You will also need speakers or a headset in order to *hear* the conference speaker. In some conferences you may be able to contribute yourself via audio, for example during Question Time at the end of a talk. If you do want to contribute, you will need a headset with microphone, rather than a stand-alone plug-in microphone or your computer's built-in microphone (if you are using a laptop). Standalone or built-in microphones frequently create echo and are not recommended for participating via voice in synchronous platforms.

The majority of online platforms used for synchronous online conferences are web-based, which means that you don't need to download any software to your computer to attend. You may need an updated version of Java installed on your computer, in which case, when you try to access the platform for the first time, the site will probably tell you what to download and where to download it from. Some platforms allow you to go to their main website – to check that your computer fulfils the requirements to be able to access the platform successfully – in advance.

The conference organisers will usually outline any software you may need to access their chosen platform, and point you in the right direction to get it, when you register for the conference. However, the majority of synchronous platforms are easy to access, and if your computer is no more than a few years old you won't need to do anything except log in and attend the conference on the day!

Further ...

Once you have 'attended' a few online conferences, the next step is to present at one! Speaking at an online conference is not the same as speaking at a face-to-face conference. Even if you are an experienced f2f conference presenter, you will need a couple of practice runs in the video-conferencing platform to be used for the online conference, to get accustomed to the interface and to learn to use the tools effectively. Conference organisers will usually offer speakers a practice session before the event so that they become familiar with the interface, learn to use any tools they need – and to ensure that the speaker's video and audio are working correctly in the chosen platform.

One thing that takes a little getting used to when presenting at an online conference is the fact that you cannot actually see or hear your audience, so it often feels as if you are speaking into a void! If the platform includes a text chat window, then participants will be able to interact with each other and with you via that channel. However, it is usually very difficult for a speaker to move through their PowerPoint slides, speak, and read the comments in the chat window at the same time! This is where having a conference moderator is key:

- The moderator can note down questions that appear in the chat window, and then relay them again at the appropriate time to the speaker.
- The moderator can also deal with any technical difficulties that participants may be having during the session, for example if a participant can't hear or see the speaker.

A word of advice: participants can find it harder to concentrate on speech for long periods of time online, even if they can see the speaker on video. They can easily leave the computer screen to go off and have a coffee, or they can simply log out! It's important to keep your online audience engaged, and this can be done not just through making sure your content is relevant and interesting, but by encouraging interaction at regular points in your online talk:

- Ask a question, or ask for a short definition of a key term related to your talk, and get the participants to type a brief response in the chat window.
- Include a very brief activity in which participants need to write on the shared whiteboard. We like to start our online talks with the outline of a world map on the whiteboard screen, and invite participants to mark where they come from, using the pen or marker function of the whiteboard.
- Round up your talk by asking participants to contribute a few adjectives to describe what they thought of it in the chat window, or to type in one thing they have learned from your session.

You can use some of the short activities that we describe for synchronous text chat tools in Part B (but make the content relevant to your talk!).

Conferences

Favourites ...

To give you an idea of the range of online conferences currently on offer in the ELT world – at the time of writing, of course – below is a short description of some of the free online conferences we have attended in the last six months, and which we thought were very good:

- **A one-hour webinar**, offered by a publisher. A well-known ELT writer spoke via video-conferencing about specific issues related to his recent book, illustrated by PowerPoint slides. He then responded verbally to questions placed by participants in the text chat. A moderator was present to introduce the webinar, to manage questions from the audience and to wrap up the session. You can find the archive of past webinars at:
  http://www.macmillanenglish.com

- **A half-day conference**, organised by a Socrates-funded European Union project. Three invited speakers spoke for approximately one hour each on ELT-related topics and ICT. Each speaker could be seen via video-conferencing, and was able to show PowerPoint slides. Participants were able to contribute and ask questions via a text chat window. There was a 15-minute break between speakers, and each speaker was introduced by a moderator, who also managed the text questions from the audience and wrapped up the session. Recordings of the conference sessions, which were held in the free video-conferencing tool Dimdim, are available here:
  http://vitaeproject.ning.com/

- **A non-stop 48-hour conference**, held in a teacher training environment within the 3-D virtual world Second Life by an online teacher training organisation. Two parallel sessions were held in separate virtual lecture spaces, with breaks between sessions, over two days. The sessions included talks and lectures with PowerPoint slides, roundtable and public discussions, virtual tours around Second Life, demo language classes, Second Life scripting and building workshops – and a lounge and disco for socialising! The annual SLanguages conference archives are available at:
  http://www.slanguages.net/home.php

- **A four-day international conference**, with invited speakers, organised by IATEFL (International Association for Teachers of English as a Foreign Language: http://www.iatefl.org). The online part of the 2010 conference, sponsored by the British Council, took place in parallel with the face-to-face conference being held in the UK. Before the conference, speakers uploaded their presentations, and discussions took place on teaching-related topics in forums. Once the f2f conference started, the f2f plenary sessions were streamed live via the online conference platform, so that participants around the world could watch these in real-time, and interact with each other via Twitter and forums. Many other conference workshops and talks were videoed and uploaded to the conference platform. There were five hours of live conference TV a day, with interviews with speakers and conference-goers. The 2010 online conference archives can be found here:
  http://iatefl.britishcouncil.org/2010/

Webinars and conferences such as those described above are regular or annual events, and we highly recommend your attending one or two, so that you experience an online seminar or conference for yourself.

Blogging

Imagine the scenario. A teacher in Moscow has her own teacher development blog. She regularly posts about what she is doing in her teaching, new ideas she is implementing or projects she is trying out with her students. She also uses the blog to reflect on what has worked and not worked in her classes, and what other teachers could do if they want to implement similar projects with their own students. She also posts examples of materials and lesson plans that she has produced.

Forms ...

As we saw in Part B, a blog is a sort of online journal or diary one regularly posts to. Posts appear in reverse chronological order, with the latest post at the top of the screen. Posts can be archived, for example by month, and you can also search a blog by keyword for a post on a particular topic. A blog has different levels of permission, and the blogger (person who blogs) can allow others to leave comments on posts, which provides a level of interaction. Bloggers often include a 'blog roll' (links to other blogs they recommend) on the main page.

You can use your blog, then, as a self-development tool – you reflect on your practice, and share your insights and ideas with other teachers via the blog. In the world of English teaching, there are many teachers who use blogs as a form of ongoing professional development. The great thing, of course, is that other teachers can access and read them and leave comments themselves, so a blog becomes a development tool which also benefits other teachers.

First ...

Before you start blogging yourself, it's a good idea to subscribe to a few teacher blogs, just so that you get a feel for the different types of blogs kept by teachers, which will help you decide what kind of blog *you* would like to set up. Even if you don't want to start blogging yourself, subscribing to a number of blogs is an excellent way to develop professionally, and to keep up with developments, debates and teaching ideas in our fields.

The best way to subscribe to a blog is via 'RSS' (Really Simple Syndication).

- Imagine that there are five different teacher blogs that you enjoy reading.
- Imagine how much time it would take you every day to go along to each of these five blogs and check whether there is anything new posted.

The alternative is to use RSS, such as Google Reader. How does it work? When you open your Google Reader page, the program goes along behind-the-scenes to the five blogs in five different websites that you have previously subscribed to. It checks whether there are any new posts and, if there are, it brings the title of the post into your Google Reader page and displays it as a list. This is all you need to do:

- Open Google Reader, look at the list of new blog post titles from the five blogs you subscribe to, and then click on any post titles that sound interesting.
- You will then be taken directly to that blog posting.

RSS saves you an enormous amount of time as the information is automatically collated and brought into your Google Reader page. Like email from discussion lists, RSS is an example of 'push' technology – information is 'pushed' directly to you, you don't need to go out and find it yourself.

Blogging

Further ...

If you feel you are now ready to move forward, there are many free blog sites on the internet, and one of the best-known is called Blogger (www.blogger.com). It is a simple process to set up a blog:

- You go along to the site, sign up for an account, then click on 'Create a blog' or similar (depending on the blog site) and you are guided through a series of screens to help you set up your blog.
- You are usually offered a choice of colours for your blog, and you can give it any name you like. Once it is set up, you are ready to start posting.

It is worth spending some time thinking about the *aim* of your blog, and who your readership will be. You can of course set up a blog for only yourself to read and not allow anybody else to read or comment on it, but that rather defeats the purpose! Blogging is a *social* activity, in which comments and input from others is welcomed. People talk about the 'blogosphere', which is the wider community of bloggers, and setting up links and networks between blogs and inviting others to visit and leave comments on your posts is part of their purpose.

Here is a list of possible aims for a teacher blog, and we provide real examples of some of these blog types in the 'Favourites' section below. Many teacher blogs will combine several aims.

- Share specific teaching ideas and materials with other teachers
- Share new tools and applications, and provide teaching ideas for other teachers
- Reflect and comment on your own teaching, and share insights gained with others
- Muse on current developments in the profession
- Invite guest writers to share their ideas/insights/opinions in the blogosphere
- Poke fun at aspects of teaching or criticise them (sometimes called 'ranting blogs')
- Comment on or discuss aspects of the English language

Favourites ...

Our favourite blogs include some which provide resources and teaching ideas for English language teachers and learners, as well as blogs that discuss issues in our field.

Nik's Learning Technologies Blog
http://nikpeachey.blogspot.com/
A resource blog. Nik Peachey regularly updates this outstanding blog for EFL teachers with 'tips, resources and teaching materials to help EFL and ESL teachers use ICT and new technology'. Posts typically look at an interesting free online tool or website, provide a brief description of it and how it works, and then provide several excellent and original teaching ideas. Posts also usually consider advantages and disadvantages of the tool, and include any relevant tips to use it more effectively. If you would like to start using a few simple ICT tools with your classes, this blog is an excellent place to start to get some teaching ideas.

Larry Ferlazzo's Websites of the Day
http://larryferlazzo.edublogs.org/about/my-best-of-series
Larry Ferlazzo is an English teacher based in California. At this blog he shares websites of interest to educators of all disciplines but especially English teachers. He has a great series of lists of websites (eg best websites for students to write their resumés, best websites for practising English pronunciation, best websites for grammar practice, and so on).

Blogging

TEFLclips

http://www.teflclips.com/

Maintained by Jamie Keddie, this resource blog provides lesson plans and ideas for teachers to use video clips from the internet in class.

An A to Z of ELT

http://scottthornbury.wordpress.com

Scott Thornbury's blog, which acts as an extension of his eponymous encyclopaedia-dictionary of language teaching (published by Macmillan). Entries are listed by letter (C is for Coursebook, E is for Error) and lively discussion and debate often follow the different entries by readers from around the world.

Carol Read's ABC of Teaching Children

http://carolread.wordpress.com

Another blog in alphabet format, the entries here are from the young learner expert. Whereas Thornbury's A to Z is in random order, Carol Read's entries follow the order of the alphabet and each one addresses an important area of young learner language education, combining theory and practical ideas.

Training ELTeachers

http://elteachertrainer.wordpress.com

John Hughes' blog ('a blog of practical ideas, thoughts and stuff for people who train teachers of ELT') is aimed at teacher trainers. It includes techniques and practical training suggestions, as well as discussions on a variety of training approaches and methodology.

DC Blog

http://david-crystal.blogspot.com

All about the English language, from David Crystal. This is what Professor Crystal himself calls a 'reactive blog', meaning that each entry is a reaction or response to a question written to him about English. It is particularly good for putting the record straight on issues such as correctness, language change and language variety – from one of the world's foremost linguists.

Six Things

http://sixthings.net/

Subtitled 'A Miscellany of English Language Teaching', this blog from Lindsay considers six things related to a range of EFL topics, from the role of technology in the classroom to the six most frequent words in English or six places for English teachers to get published. Some topics are light-hearted, some more serious. A good place for keeping up with current debates in the field.

eModeration Station

http://www.emoderationskills.com

Nicky maintains this blog, which consists of 'tools, techniques, tips and tweets' for online tutors (or 'e-moderators'). Aimed at online educators from any discipline, it contains plenty of useful tips for online language teachers and online teacher trainers. Topics include: tips on how to moderate or present a webinar, discussions of best practice in online learning, posts on innovations in language teaching (such as 'mobile learning' or teaching with handheld devices), and so on.

Micro-blogging

Micro-blogging, or 'blogging for lazy people', is a fairly recent internet-based phenomenon, at least compared to traditional blogging, which has been around since about 1997. Micro-blogging tools such as Twitter (http://twitter.com) are being used by professional communities for professional development in many walks of life, and EFL teaching is certainly no exception.

Forms ...

How does micro-blogging work, and what is it? Let's take the example of Twitter, currently one of the best-known micro-blogging tools. Twitter is a web-based application, in which you can type a short message (known as a 'tweet') with a maximum of 140 characters (not words!) and send it to your contacts. The basic idea is for people to simply answer the question 'What are you doing?' several times a day, and to send this out to their Twitter network. So it's a bit like sending an SMS update on your movements to a large group of friends at the same time.

How can Twitter help teachers with professional development? Once you have joined Twitter and created your Twitter network (see 'First' below for how to do this), you can start to tweet. You do need to have a critical mass of about 50 people in your network, to start to experience the benefits of Twitter. In the English language teaching and training world, there are already extensive Twitter networks in existence.

What do EFL and ESL teachers tweet about? Typically, you will see tweets on a variety of topics: links to interesting articles, comments, news, information related to our field, and personal comments. Of course, the content you receive in tweets depends on who is in your network (or who you 'follow' – in Twitter parlance)!

First ...

The best way to get started is to sign up and open an account on http://twitter.com – you need to log in to Twitter to be able to receive and read messages – and to find people to add to your network, or to follow. The easiest way to find people in the ELT field to follow is to look at a couple of well-known individuals in the profession, to look at their contact list (or 'followers') and simply start to follow the same people. Once you're following somebody:

- You will receive any messages that they send out via Twitter.
- These messages appear on your own Twitter page.

You yourself will need to have followers, if people are going to receive *your* messages – in the Twittersphere (or world of Twitter), people whom *you* start to follow will often return the favour by following *you* and, in this way, you can gradually build up your network of people you receive messages from (the people you follow) and people who will receive your messages (your own followers).

Further ...

Once you have belonged to Twitter for a while, and have got an idea of the sorts of messages people post, you could start posting your own messages to your own followers. Interesting and useful messages are often 're-tweeted' – that is, one of your followers might decide to resend (or re-tweet) your message to their own network, to help spread the word.

Micro-blogging

A word of advice: the ethos of the Twittersphere is such that commercial messages are frowned upon, and should be avoided if you want to keep your followers!

It may take a little while to start to see the point of Twitter, or to make it work effectively for you. We suggest the following:

- Log in at least daily for about a month, once you have your critical mass of about 50 people to follow.
- You can then see to what extent you find the tweets of your followers interesting and useful.

To start to build up your own network, you could follow Nicky and Lindsay on Twitter. We are both are avid tweeters! Once you have set up your own Twitter account, search for Nicky and Lindsay via your Twitter page. Click on 'Find people', and enter their Twitter usernames.

- This is Nicky's: @theconsultantse
- This is Lindsay's: @lclandfield

Then go to our profiles, look at who *we* are following, and choose some of the same people to follow.

There are also ways to start using Twitter with your own learners, and if you google a phrase like 'twitter with students' or 'twitter tips for students' you should find a number of links that will take you to suggestions and ideas for using this micro-blogging tool with classroom and online learners.

Favourites ...

There are a number of mico-blogging tools on the internet, and more are appearing all the time. Below are the two we currently find most useful:

- One for our own professional development
- One for use with learners

Twitter
http://twitter.com
We find Twitter especially useful for our own professional development. Following a wide range of people involved in ELT and, equally, having a good number of followers means that you can be constantly involved in a community which is communicating in real-time, exhanging ideas, links, insights, comments – and more.

Edmodo
http://www.edmodo.com
This is another micro-blogging tool, known as 'Twitter for education'. We personally find Edmodo more effective than Twitter for using with groups of learners or teacher trainees. Whereas Twitter requires following and being followed by individuals, making it time-consuming to set up a personal network, an Edmodo 'class' or group can be set up by the teacher, and an 'entry key' (password) simply sent to learners so that everybody can access the same Edmodo space easily and be instantly connected.

It also allows for the sharing of multimedia files, links, assignments, deadlines and polls. Its groups or classes can remain private – only those with the access key can join – and you can set up as many separate groups as you like. As you can see: a wealth of advantages.

ePortfolios

A 'portfolio' is a collection of work so, unsurprisingly, an 'ePortfolio' is a collection of work in electronic format. It is more flexible than a paper-based portfolio, allowing for a range of digital media to be included – such as video, audio, blogs, and links to websites.

Forms ...

In the teaching profession and in many disciplines, ePortfolios are increasingly being used to present and assess both adult and young learners' work in electronic format. Teachers can also create an ePortfolio, either as a developmental tool or as a 'showcase' of their best practice.

- They can be *ongoing* and *developmental* – that is, the ePortfolio is compiled over time and can show development.
- They can be a *finished product* or *'summative'*, and show examples of best work. This kind of showcase portfolio can then be used by a learner to seek employment, or as proof of language proficiency and skills.

In this section, we explore how teachers can set up their own ePortfolio. This is a necessary first step if you are planning to try using an ePortfolio with your learners. You should first learn how to set one up yourself – before you ask learners to do so!

First ...

When planning your own teacher ePortfolio, there are a number of basic questions you first need to ask yourself:

- Who is the intended audience of your ePortfolio? In other words, who is going to read it, and why?
- Are you planning to use it as a *developmental* tool, with work in process and accompanying reflections, or is it going to be a *showcase* portfolio, which only includes examples of your best practice?
- What sort of content are you going to include?
- What tool are you going to use? (See the 'Favourites' section on page 107.)
- How are you going to share and distribute your ePortfolio, especially if you're using it to seek employment? Online via a link? On a CD/DVD?
- Are you going to keep your ePortfolio completely private, so that only those with permission will be able to view it online? Or will it be publicly available?

Further ...

Whether developmental or showcase, a language teacher ePortfolio will typically include an outline of your beliefs about teaching (your teaching philosophy), your teaching experience and any relevant qualifications, examples of lesson plans, syllabi and/or tests produced, and even some sample course materials, including multimedia (your own blogs, or blogs you've set up with your learners, podcasts, etc). Some teachers' ePortfolios include evidence of teaching effectiveness, such as video recordings of sample classes, samples of learners' work (included in the ePortfolio, with their permissions of course), learner feedback and possibly even departmental evaluations.

A showcase ePortfolio can also include any teaching awards, and publications such as articles that you have produced. Finally, you can include professional development that you have taken part in, such as courses, conferences attended, talks and workshops you have given, and any other professional development tools that you use or have created, such as any of those explored in Part C.

If you are creating a showcase portfolio, once you have set it up and added your content you shouldn't need to update it more than a couple of times a year. You want to keep your showcase portfolio looking as attractive as possible, so include a photo of yourself, and images that are relevant to the content.

If you are providing a link to a video project example, embed the video into the portfolio page rather than simply providing a link – it will look far more attractive (and professional) that way. Simply google 'how to embed video into [name of tool]' to find out how to do this.

Make sure that the portfolio content is separated into clear and logical sections, and that the content itself is easy to read and not too long. If you are including lengthy reports or articles, it's better to keep these on separate links away from the main portfolio page.

Favourites ...

To see examples of publicly available teachers' ePortfolios on the internet, try googling 'teacher ePortfolio' and follow some of the links. We can't recommend any teachers' ePortfolios by name. However:

- The best ones are very clearly laid out, with different pages for different sections of the ePortfolio.
- They have a very clear aim and purpose.

Good showcase ePortfolios also clearly show the teacher's experience, qualifications and contact details, and will contain sample work in many of the areas outlined in 'Further' above.

Which are the best tools with which to set up an ePortfolio?

For developmental and/or showcase ePortfolios, we highly recommend using the free online Cambridge ESOL Teacher Portfolios: https://www.teacherportfolio.cambridgeesol.org/

We suggest starting with a tool such as this one – it simply requires you to log in and to fill in or add information online, so you don't need to set anything up from scratch. Apart from the clear organisation of this portfolio tool, there is also a print version, perfect for sending to prospective employers if you prefer to have a paper version of your portfolio.

Other tools you could use to create an ePortfolio include:

- Wikis such as:
  Wikispaces (http://www.wikispaces.com)
  PBWorks (http://pbworks.com)
  WetPaint (http://www.wetpaint.com)
- More complex online portfolio tools such as Mahara (http://mahara.org), which can be integrated into Moodle
- Social networking tools such as Elgg (http://elgg.org), which can be adapted to the purposes of a developmental ePortfolio

This last group of tools requires a little more know-how, as you need to set them all up yourself. However, many of them are very easy to set up and use, and some have demo videos in the site to help you. A WetPaint wiki/ePortfolio, particularly, is very easy to create, and probably a good place to start if you would like to design your own ePortfolio from the word go.

Personal Learning Networks

As we have seen in Part C, there are many ways that, as teachers, we can take advantage of the internet in order to develop professionally. However, with so much on offer (and so much of it for free!), you may be asking some of these questions:

- Where to start?
- What teacher development tools should you start using?
- How can you get an overview of what you *already* do, what you feel you *should* do, and what you *want* to do next – for your own professional and personal development?

A term that is being increasingly used to refer to the way we integrate many sources of information and communication into our personal and professional development is that of 'Personal Learning Network' or 'PLN'. You may also hear the term 'Personal Learning Environment (PLE) to talk about the same thing.

Forms ...

A Personal Learning Network does what it suggests: it consists of a *network* of sources, resources and options which will contribute to your own personal learning. In this sense, it is not a tool, website or program – rather, it is a series of *options* that you put together in the way that suits you best. The easiest way to understand a PLN is to visualise it. Nicky's PLN looks like this:

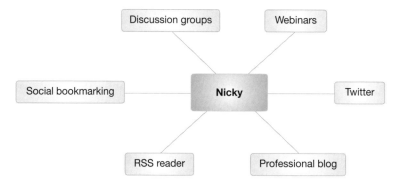

We can fill out more details from the diagram:

- Nicky belongs to several email-based discussion groups.
- She tries to attend webinars (or online seminars) about once a fortnight.
- She regularly uses Twitter to share and learn about new resources by logging in, on average, once a day.
- She keeps her own professional blog, in which she reflects on technology and online teaching.
- She has an RSS reader that enables her to subscribe to around 50 blogs, but she doesn't visit or read them all every day! She reads a few blog posts a day, and comments on one or two of these a few times a week.
- She keeps track of interesting new websites and resources by 'bookmarking' them (or saving them) online in Delicious, her social bookmarking tool of choice: http://delicious.com. By keeping them bookmarked online, she can access them from any computer, from her smartphone, and even share them with her network of colleagues.

Personal Learning Networks

First ...

Take a moment to reflect on your own PLN. Are there any elements that you already have in your own PLN?

- You may already belong to an online teacher discussion group.
- You may visit websites or blogs to get ideas and activities to use in your own classes.

These are already elements of *your* PLN. How, then, to proceed from here?

- Create a blank mindmap. You can do this on paper or by using a free mindmapping tool online, such as those we recommend on page 23.
- Fill in the things you already do for your own professional development. These may be things that you do online and things that you do face-to-face (such as attending workshops in your school or town).

Further ...

Now add some more blank areas to your mindmap, and fill in a few new professional development ideas, from those that we have explored in Part C and from the range of Options and Opportunities on page 110.

- Mark these new areas in order of priority for you.
- Mark which ones you would like to try first, and those you would like to try later. Perhaps add deadline dates for trying each option.
- You can now start to explore these new areas slowly over the coming term or year!

And further ...

A Personal Learning Network is a developing network, not a static network. Your PLN should evolve over time, organically. As you explore new ways of learning, they are incorporated. You may find some of the options don't work that well for you, and decide to drop them. Everybody's PLN will be different:

- What development options suit *you* best?
- What do *you* find most interesting or useful?

Your PLN is a work in progress, a developing and flexible network of options and opportunities, not a project to 'get done'. You will see that the diagram elaborated on our final page does not present a 'closed' list.

There will always be 'Other' possibilities for your online development. Although Part C has focused exclusively on *online* development opportunities, we mustn't forget that there may also exist *face-to-face* opportunities in your teaching context – attending local conferences, attending in-house teacher development sessions or simply holding regular meetings with other teachers in which you prepare materials together.

Other online possibilities for your own professional development will no doubt emerge in the future, with new tools and applications appearing all the time. Who, for example, could have predicted even a few years ago that a micro-blogging tool like Twitter would come along and be so useful for professional development?

We hope, then, that your Personal Learning Network will continue to expand and help you to continue learning – for the rest of your professional life.

Options and opportunities

Here are just some options to try out, to get you started with creating your own PLN.
They are presented under the headings in which we looked at each one in Part C.
You don't need to do all of them – just choose one or two at first!

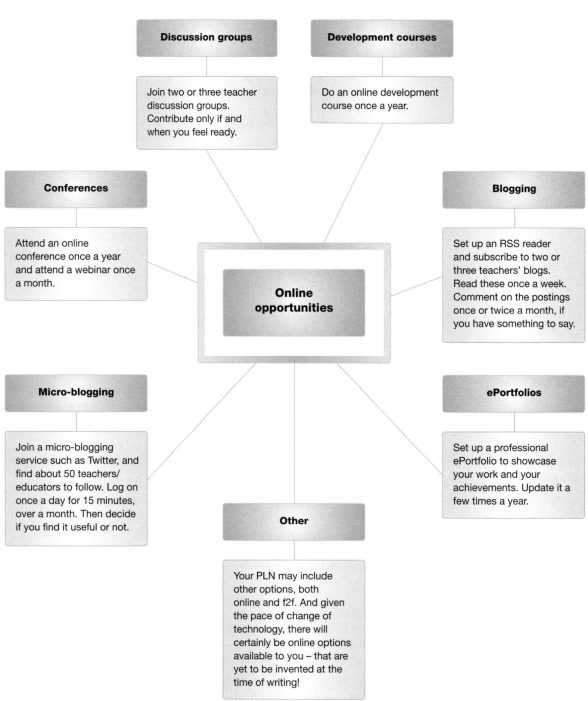

Discussion groups

Join two or three teacher discussion groups. Contribute only if and when you feel ready.

Development courses

Do an online development course once a year.

Conferences

Attend an online conference once a year and attend a webinar once a month.

Blogging

Set up an RSS reader and subscribe to two or three teachers' blogs. Read these once a week. Comment on the postings once or twice a month, if you have something to say.

Online opportunities

Micro-blogging

Join a micro-blogging service such as Twitter, and find about 50 teachers/ educators to follow. Log on once a day for 15 minutes, over a month. Then decide if you find it useful or not.

ePortfolios

Set up a professional ePortfolio to showcase your work and your achievements. Update it a few times a year.

Other

Your PLN may include other options, both online and f2f. And given the pace of change of technology, there will certainly be online options available to you – that are yet to be invented at the time of writing!

From the editor

Teaching Online is a clear, accessible and reassuringly practical book for all those teachers who are venturing into online course delivery. Nicky Hockly and Lindsay Clandfield have taught extensively on courses that are both fully online and 'blended'.

The time had come to share this wealth of experience – through a combination of theory, practice and paths for professional development.

- What you need to get started
- How you can get going and build your own online course
- The essentials of successful online teaching, from course sites to course behaviour
- A comprehensive list of tools for teaching online, from blogs to word clouds

- Practical activities with step-by-step instructions – what you need and what you do
- Activities that cover the four skills – as well as language work and evaluation
- Special sections for activities to begin and finish an online course
- Comments on how to make your online teaching more effective

- Avenues for online teacher development
- Web 2.0 tools that connect with a worldwide community of teachers
- References to the authors' own favourite sites and tools for development
- The concept of the PLN (Personal Learning Network) for teachers

Teaching Online is an important first in ELT and a must for any teacher thinking of expanding their horizons, providing both the tools and the techniques for online language instruction.

The world of online teaching isn't a science fiction scenario of the future of education. It's here and it's now.

Mike Burghall

From the publisher

DELTA TEACHER DEVELOPMENT SERIES

A pioneering new series of books for English Language Teachers
with professional development in mind.

Teaching Online
by Nicky Hockly with Lindsay Clandfield
ISBN 978-1-905085-35-4

Culture in our Classrooms
by Gill Johnson and Mario Rinvolucri
ISBN 978-1-905085-21-7

The Developing Teacher
by Duncan Foord
ISBN 978-1-905085-22-4

The Business English Teacher
by Debbie Barton, Jennifer Burkart
and Caireen Sever
ISBN 978-1-905085-34-7

Being Creative
by Chaz Pugliese
ISBN 978-1-905085-33-0

Teaching Unplugged
by Luke Meddings and Scott Thornbury
ISBN 978-1-905085-19-4

For details of future titles in the series,
please contact the publisher or visit the DTDS website at
www.deltapublishing.co.uk/titles/methodology/delta-teacher-development-series

---

Also from DELTA PUBLISHING

professional perspectives

A series of practical methodology books designed to provide teachers of English
with fresh insights, innovative ideas and original classroom materials.

Creating Conversation in Class
by Chris Sion
ISBN 978-0-953309-88-7

Challenging Children
by Henk van Oort
ISBN 978-1-900783-93-4

Dealing with Difficulties
by Luke Prodromou and Lindsay Clandfield
ISBN 978-1-905085-00-2

Humanising your Coursebook
by Mario Rinvolucri
ISBN 978-0-954198-60-2

Spontaneous Speaking
by David Heathfield
ISBN 978-1-900783-92-7

Talking Business in Class
by Chris Sion
ISBN 978-1-900783-64-4

The MINIMAX Teacher
by Jon Taylor
ISBN 978-0953309-89-4

The Resourceful English Teacher
by Jonathan Chandler and Mark Stone
ISBN 978-0-953309-81-8

Unlocking Self-expression through NLP
by Judith Baker and Mario Rinvolucri
ISBN 978-1-900783-88-0

Using the Mother Tongue
by Sheelagh Deller and Mario Rinvolucri
ISBN 978-0-954198-61-9

Please contact the publisher for further details:
Tel +44 (0)1306 731770   *E-mail* info@deltapublishing.co.uk
Web www.deltapublishing.co.uk